HAIKU AND MODERNIST POETICS

HAIKU AND MODERNIST POETICS

Yoshinobu Hakutani

First published in 2009 by PALGRAVE MACMILLAN®
in the United States—a division of St. Martin's Press LLC,
175 Fifth Avenue, New York, NY 10010.

Where this book is distributed in the UK, Europe and the rest of
the world, this is by Palgrave Macmillan, a division of Macmillan
Publishers Limited, registered in England, company number 785998,
of Houndmills, Basingstoke, Hampshire RG21 6XS.

Palgrave Macmillan is the global academic imprint of the above
companies and has companies and representatives throughout the
world.

Palgrave® and Macmillan® are registered trademarks in the United
States, the United Kingdom, Europe and other countries.

ISBN: 978-0-230-61655-4

Library of Congress Cataloging-in-Publication Data is available from
the Library of Congress.

A catalogue record of the book is available from the British Library.

Design by Scribe Inc.

First edition: September 2009

10 9 8 7 6 5 4 3 2 1

Printed in the United States of America.

To Michiko Watanabe Hakutani

CONTENTS

ACKNOWLEDGMENTS

I am indebted to many writers and sources, as acknowledged in the notes and works cited. I would like to thank, in particular, the late John M. Reilly, Keiichi Harada, Robert L. Tener, Robert James Butler, and Michiko Watanabe Hakutani, who have read part or all of the manuscript and offered useful, constructive suggestions.

Over the years the Kent State University Research Council has provided several research leaves and travel grants, and I am grateful for their support.

I have used in modified form my previously published essays "Yone Noguchi's Poetry: From Whitman to Zen" (*Comparative Literature Studies*, 1985); "Ezra Pound, Yone Noguchi, and Imagism" (*Modern Philology*, 1992); "W. B. Yeats, Modernity, and the Noh Play" in *Modernity in East-West Literary Criticism: New Readings* (Associated University Presses, 2001); "Cross-Cultural Poetics: Sonia Sanchez's *Like the Singing Coming off the Drums*" and "James Emanuel's Jazz Haiku and African American Individualism" in *Cross-Cultural Visions in African American Modernism: From Spatial Narrative to Jazz Haiku* (Ohio State University Press, 2006); and "Richard Wright's Haiku, Zen, and the African 'Primal Outlook upon Life'" (*Modern Philology*, 2007).

INTRODUCTION

Haiku, the Japanese verse of seventeen syllables, was derived from the *waka* (Japanese song), the oldest verse form of thirty-one syllables, written vertically in five parts (5-7-5-7-7). As an amusement at the court, one poet composed the first three parts (5-7-5) of a *waka* and another poet was challenged to provide the last two (7-7) to complete the verse. The haiku form thus corresponds to the first three parts of the *waka*. This seventeen-syllable verse form had been preserved by noblemen, courtiers, and high-ranked samurai since the thirteenth century. Around the beginning of the sixteenth century, haiku became popular among the poets. Haiku, called *hokku* (starting verse) at that time, was also a dominant element of another popular verse form, *renga* (linked song).

By 1680, when Matsuo Basho (1644–94) wrote the first version of his celebrated haiku on the frog jumping into the water, haiku had become a highly stylized expression of poetic vision:

> Furu ike ya
> Kawazu tobi komu
> Mizu no oto

> [The old pond:
> A frog jumped into
> The sound of the water.]

Basho's haiku, unlike those of his predecessors, represented a new perspective and did not rely on the ingenious play on words often seen in *renga*. Basho, his contemporaries, and the later masters such as Yosa Buson (1716–83) and Kobayashi Issa (1763–1827) attempted to write the serious haiku, a unique poetic genre that was short but was able to offer more than wit or humor. Because of their brevity and condensation, haiku seldom provide details. The haiku poet draws only an outline or a highly selective image, and the reader must complete the vision. Above all, a classic haiku, as opposed to a modernist one, is required to include a clear reference to one of the four seasons.

The philosophy that underlies much of classic haiku is Zen. A haiku poet like Basho strived to create a vision in which nature and humanity are united. Such a poet sought to suppress his individuality and achieve the state of Zen, of what R. H. Blyth calls "absolute spiritual poverty in which, having nothing, we possess all." In Zen-inspired haiku, the material or the concrete is emphasized without the expression of any general principles of abstract reasoning. In traditional haiku, animate and inanimate lose their differences, so that one might say haiku are not about human beings but about objects in nature. Zen teaches that the ordinary thing and the love of nature are reduced to a detached love of life as it is, without idealistic, moralistic, or ethical attachments. Things in nature are equal to human beings; both exist through and because of each other. In a Zen-inspired haiku, the poet tries to annihilate one's thoughts or feelings before satori is attained. Satori is the achievement of a state of *mu*, nothingness. The state of nothingness is free of human subjectivity; it is so completely free of any thought or emotion that such a consciousness corresponds to the state of nature.

Among the modernists in the twentieth century, Yone Noguchi (1875–1947) played the most vital role in disseminating Japanese poetics and haiku, in particular, to the West. As early as 1903 he met W. B. Yeats in London; in the 1920s and 1930s, Noguchi was the best-known interpreter of Japanese art in the West, especially in England. Beginning with *The Spirit of Japanese Art*, he published ten books about celebrated artists, with colorful illustrations, on Hiroshige, Korin, Utamaro, Hokusai, and Harunobu. Yeats, whose interest in the *noh* play is well known, became fascinated with these artists through Noguchi. Noguchi in return dedicated the collection of his own English haiku to Yeats.

Through Yeats and other English writers, Noguchi also became well acquainted with Ezra Pound as early as 1911. In the meantime Noguchi's later poetry, collected in *The Pilgrimage* and *Japanese Hokkus*, and his literary criticism, *The Spirit of Japanese Poetry*, in particular, were widely circulated in the West. Noguchi played a principal role in relating Japanese poetics to Western intentions in early modernism. Among the various sources of influence and assimilation, the Imagists responded directly to the example of their fellow poet Noguchi. In Japan, on the other hand, his associations with poets in the West had a considerable impact on such modernist Japanese poets as Shimazaki Toson (1872–1943), Takamura Kotaro (1883–1952), and Hagiwara Sakutaro (1886–1942).

In his essay "Vorticism," published in *The Fortnightly Review* in 1914, Pound acknowledged for the first time in his career his indebtedness to Japanese poetics in general and the art of haiku in particular. In this essay his famous haiku-like poem, "In a Station of the Metro," appeared. In the same essay Pound also quoted Moritake's haiku, "The fallen blossoms flies to its branch: A butterfly," just before discussing his "In a Station of the Metro." To demonstrate his theory of imagism, Pound thought of an image not as a decorative emblem or symbol but as a seed capable of germinating and developing into another organism. To Pound, another equally important tenet of imagism called for directness in expression. The immediate model for this principle was nineteenth-century French prose. He seemed strongly opposed to Victorian poetry, which he characterized as wordy and rhetorical. If Pound's ideal poetry had the directness and clarity of good prose in contrast to the suggestiveness and vagueness of symbolist poetry, his sources certainly did not include Yeats. Even though Yeats dedicated his *noh* play *At the Hawk's Well* to Pound, Yeats was not enthusiastic about Pound's modernist poetics. The difference between Pound and Yeats revealed itself in the two modernist poets' differing views of the Japanese *noh* play. A symbolist and spiritualist poet, Yeats was fascinated by the *noh* play, which stages not a realistic and elaborate but a symbolic and spiritual setting, while Pound, an Imagist, was interested not in particular images and symbols but in the unifying effect a *noh* play produces on the stage.

During the early decades of the twentieth century, few books had been published on haiku. The end of World War II, however, provoked an outpouring of interest in Japanese haiku. In the late 1940s and 1950s, a number of important books in English on haiku were published. Among them, R. H. Blyth's four volumes of Japanese haiku with his translations and analyses inspired many Americans to write haiku in English. Many poets of the Beat Generation, most notably Allen Ginsberg (1926–97), Jack Kerouac (1922–69), and Gary Snyder (1930–), tried their hand at composing haiku. Kerouac, who had captured a huge audience when his first book, *On the Road*, appeared in 1958, wrote numerous haiku throughout his career and played a central role in the literary movement he named the Beat Generation. His second novel, *The Dharma Bums* (1958), gave an intimate biographical account of himself in search of the truth in life. In San Francisco he met Gary Snyder, and the two so-called Dharma bums explored the thoughts and practices of Buddhism. As Snyder left for Japan to study at a Zen monastery, Kerouac reached an apogee on a desolate mountaintop in the Sierras. Through his friendship with such Beat poets as Snyder and Ginsberg, as well as through his studies of Buddhism, Zen, and R. H. Blyth's volume *Haiku: Eastern Culture* in particular, Kerouac firmly established his poetics. His haiku reflected his fascination with Mahayana Buddhism, as well as with Zen philosophy. What is remarkable about his haiku is that not only was he influenced by the books he read, but he was also inspired by his own experience in wandering and meditating in the fields and on the mountains.

The most influential East-West artistic, cultural, and literary exchange that has taken place in modern and postmodern times was reading and writing of haiku in the West. Among others in the West, Richard Wright (1908–60) distinguished himself as a haiku poet by writing more than 4,000 haiku in the last eighteen months of his life while in exile in Paris. In 1955 Wright attended the Bandung Conference of the Third World; two years later he was a member of the First Congress of Negro Artists and Writers, which met in Paris in September 1957. During that same period he liked to work in the garden on his Normandy farm, an activity that supplied many themes for his haiku. Of his experience in this period, Wright's travel to the newly independent nation of Ghana in West Africa had a great impact on his writing of haiku. The African philosophy of life that Wright witnessed among the Ashanti—"the African primal outlook upon life" as he called it—served as an inspiration for his poetic sensibility. Ezra Pound's theory that the poet's use of an image is not to support "some system of ethics or economics" coincides with a theory that haiku expresses the poet's intuitive worldview. Wright, then, found the haiku poet's intuitive worldview akin to that of the African.

Since 1998, when Wright's posthumous *Haiku: This Other World* was published, Wright's haiku have made an immediate impact on some contemporary American poets, most notably Robert Haas (1941–), Sonia Sanchez (1935–), and James A. Emanuel (1921–). Haas, the U. S. poet laureate from 1995 to 1997, wrote in the *Washington Post*, "Here's a surprise, a book of haiku written in his last years by the fierce and original American novelist Richard Wright. . . . What an outpouring!" There appeared numerous reviews praising Wright's unexpected achievement, such as "*Haiku: This Other World* is an outstanding addition to Wright's literary and humanist achievements and stands as a beacon to this other world" (*The Japan Times*), and "The only full collection of haiku by a major American writer to remotely suggest both the range and depth possible in the genre" (*The Santa Fe News*).

As some of the haiku and *tanka* (short song) collected in *Like the Singing Coming off the Drums* (1998) reflect, Sonia Sanchez follows the poetic tradition in which human action emulates nature and the poet suppresses human subjectivity. In portraying nature, Sanchez is at times puzzled by its spontaneous imagery. In such poems she is reluctant to draw a distinction between human beings and animals, animate and inanimate objects. Not only do many of Sanchez's haiku follow Zen doctrine, but they also share the aesthetic principles that underlie classic haiku, such as *yugen*, by which to express the sense of loss. From time to time, her blues haiku figure a brightened sense of *yugen*. As aesthetic principles, *yugen* and the blues share the sentiments derived from private and intensely personal feelings. Unlike *yugen*, the blues in Sanchez's haiku confines its attention solely to the immediate and celebrates the bodily expression. Most importantly, Sanchez tries to link the blues message with sexually charged language so as to liberate black bodies from the distorted images that slavery inflicted.

In *Jazz from the Haiku King* (1999), James A. Emanuel tries to fuse haiku with jazz. His intention is to translate the musical expressions of African American life, its pain and joy, into the 5-7-5 syllabic measure of haiku. In so doing, he has also attempted to expand the imagery of the traditional haiku beyond its simple impression by including narrative and rhyme. On the surface, jazz and haiku have much in common. As jazz performance thrives on an endless improvisation that the composer fashions from traditional materials, such as spirituals and the blues, so does haiku composition thrive on an infinite improvisation with beautiful objects in nature and humanity. In the process, the composer in both genres must efface one's identity and subjectivity. In jazz, play changes on ideas as well as on sounds to create unexpected sensations. In haiku, the poet spares no pains to capture unexpected sensations. In both genres the composer and the composed, subject and object, coalesce as the identity of the composer disappears in the wake of creation. As Zen stresses self-reliance, not egotism, nature, not materialism, so does jazz. Just as jazz challenges us to hear sounds and rhythms we have not heard before, so does haiku challenge us to see images of nature and humanity we have not seen before. For Emanuel, a postmodern and postcolonial poet, haiku and jazz enable us to open our minds and imagine ways of reaching a higher ground in our present lives.

CHAPTER 1

THE GENESIS AND DEVELOPMENT
OF HAIKU IN JAPAN

Like transcendentalists such as Emerson and Whitman, Japanese haiku poets were inspired by nature, especially its beautiful scenes and seasonal changes. Poetry by Emerson and Whitman has an affinity with Japanese haiku in terms of its attitude toward nature. Although the exact origin of haiku is not clear, the close relationship that haiku has with nature suggests the ways in which the ancient Japanese people lived on those islands. Where they came from is unknown, but they must have adapted their living to ways of nature. Many were farmers, others hunters, fishermen, and warriors. While they often confronted nature, they always tried to live in harmony with it: Buddhism and Shintoism constantly taught them that the soul existed in them as well as in nature, the animate and the inanimate alike, and that nature must be preserved as much as possible. Haiku traditionally avoided such subjects as earthquakes, floods, illnesses, and eroticism—ugly aspects of nature. Instead, haiku poets were attracted to such objects as flowers, trees, birds, sunset, the moon, and genuine love. Those who earned their livelihood by labor had to battle with the negative aspects of nature, but noblemen, priests, writers, singers, and artists found beauty and pleasure in natural phenomena. Since the latter group of people had the time to idealize or romanticize nature and impose a philosophy on it, they became an elite group of Japanese culture. Basho was an essayist, Buson a painter, and Issa a Buddhist priest, as well as each being an accomplished haiku poet.

The genesis of haiku can be seen in the *waka* (Japanese song), the oldest verse form of thirty-one syllables in five lines (5-7-5-7-7), mentioned in the introduction. The first three lines of the *waka* are arranged 5-7-5, with such exceptions as 5-7-6 and 5-8-5. *Hyakunin Isshu* (*One Hundred Poems by One Hundred Poets*), a *waka* anthology compiled by Fujiwara no Sadaiye (1162–1241) in 1235 contains haiku-like verses. Sadaiye's "Chiru Hana wo" ("The Falling Blossoms"), for example, reads,

> Chiru hana wo
> Oikakete yuku
> Arashi kana

· (Henderson 10)

> [The falling blossoms:
> Look at them, it is the storm
> That is chasing them.[1]]

The focus of this verse is the poet's observation of a natural object, the falling blossoms. To a beautiful picture Sadaiye adds his feeling about this phenomenon: it looks as though a storm is pursuing the falling flower petals.

This seventeen-syllable-verse form had been preserved by noblemen, courtiers, and high-ranked samurai for over two centuries since the publication of *Hyakunin Isshu*. As noted in the introduction, around the beginning of the sixteenth century the verse form became popular among the poets. It was a dominant element of another popular verse form, *renga* (linked song), a continuous chain of fourteen (7-7) and seventeen (5-7-5) syllable verses, each independently composed but connected as one poem. The first collection of *renga*, *Chikuba Kyogin Shu* (*Chikuba Singers' Collection*, 1499) contains over two hundred *tsukeku* (adding verses) linked with the first verses of another poet. As the word *kyogin* in the title of this collection suggests, renga verses are generally characterized by a display of ingenuity and coarse humor. *Chikuba Kyogin Shu* also collected twenty *hokku* (starting verse). Because the *hokku* was considered the most important verse of a *renga* series, it was usually composed by the senior poet attending a *renga* session. The fact that this collection included a much fewer number of *hokku* in proportion to *tsukeku* indicates the poets' interest in the comic nature of the *renga*.[2]

By the time Matsuo Basho (1644–94) wrote that famous poem on the frog jumping into the old pond, as noted in the introduction, *haikai*, an older poetic genre from which haiku evolved, had become

a unique expression of poetic vision. Basho's poem was totally different from most of the *haikai* poems written by his predecessors: it was
the creation of a new perception and not merely an ingenious play on
words. As most scholars observe, the changes and innovations brought
about in *haikai* poetry were not accomplished by a single poet.[3] Basho's
contemporaries, with Basho as their leader, attempted to create the serious *haikai*, a verse form known in modern times as haiku.[4] The haiku,
then, was a highly uncommon genre that was short but could give more
than wit or humor: a haiku late in the seventeenth century became a
crystallized expression of one's vision and sensibility.

Because of their brevity and condensation, haiku seldom provides
the picture with detail. The haiku poet delineates only an outline or
highly selective parts, and the reader must complete the vision. Above
all, a classic haiku, as opposed to a modern one, is required to include
a clear reference to one of the four seasons, as noted earlier. In Basho's
"The Old Pond," said to be written in the spring of 1686, a seasonal
reference to spring is made by the frog in the second line: the plunging
of a single frog into the deep water suddenly breaks the deadly quiet
background. Although the frog is traditionally a *kigo* (seasonal word)
of spring, some critics have considered this haiku evokes a scene in
autumn, because it draws at once a picture of an autumnal desolation
reigning over an ancient temple pond. As a result, the poet's perception of the infinitely quiet universe is intensified. It is also imperative
that a haiku be primarily concerned with nature; if a haiku deals with
human life, that life must be viewed in the context of nature rather
than society.

The predilection to portray human life in association with nature
means that the poet is more interested in genuinely human sentiments
than in moral, ethical, or political problems. The following haiku by
Kaga no Chiyo (1703–75), a famous woman poet in her age, illustrates
that haiku thrives on the affinity between humanity and nature:

> Asagao ni
> Tsurube torarete
> Morai mizu[5]

> [A morning glory
> Has taken the well bucket:
> I'll borrow water.]

Since a fresh, beautiful morning glory has grown on her well bucket
overnight, Chiyo does not mind going over to her neighbor's to borrow

water. Not only does her action show a desire to preserve nature, but the poem also expresses a natural and tender feeling one has for nature. A classic haiku, while it shuns human-centered emotions, thrives on such a nature-centered feeling as Chiyo's. This sensibility cannot be explained by logic or reason. Longer poems are often filled with intellectualized or moralized reasoning, but haiku avoids such language.

Because haiku is limited in its length, it must achieve its effect by a sense of unity and harmony within. Feelings of unity and harmony, indicative of Zen philosophy, are motivated by a desire to perceive every instant in nature and life: an intuition that nothing is alone, nothing is out of the ordinary. The unity of sentiment in haiku is intensified by the poet's expression of the senses. The transference of the senses may occur between color and mood, as shown in a haiku by Usuda Aro, a contemporary Japanese poet:

> Tsuma araba
> Tozomou asagao
> Akaki saku[6]

> [Were my wife alive,
> I thought, and saw a morning glory:
> It has blossomed red.]

The first line conveys a feeling of loneliness, but the red morning glory reminds him of a happy life they spent when she was living. The redness, rather than the whiteness or blue color of the flower, is transferred to the feeling of happiness and love. The transference of the senses, in turn, arouses a sense of balance and harmony. His recollection of their happy marriage, a feeling evoked by the red flower, compensates for the death of his wife, a reality.

Well-wrought haiku thrive on the fusion of humanity and nature and on the intensity of love and beauty it creates. A haiku by Takarai Kikaku (1661–1707), Basho's first disciple and one of the more innovative poets, is exemplary:

> Meigetsu ya
> Tatami no ue ni
> Matsu no kage[7]

> [The harvest moon:
> Lo, on the tatami mats
> The shape of a pine.]

The beauty of the moonlight here is not only humanized, since the light is shining on the human-made object, but also intensified by the shadows of a pine tree that fall on the mats. The beauty of the shadow reflected on the human-made object is far more luminous than the light itself, for the intricate pattern of an ageless pine tree as it stamps the dustless mats intensifies the beauty of the moonlight. Not only does such a scene unify the image of humanity and that of nature, but humanity and nature also interact.

As haiku has developed over the centuries, it has established certain aesthetic principles, as mentioned in the introduction. To define and illustrate them is difficult since they refer to subtle perceptions and complex states of mind in the creation of poetry. Above all, these principles are governed by the national character developed over the centuries. Having changed in meaning, they do not necessarily mean the same today as they did in the seventeenth century. Discussion of these terms, furthermore, proves difficult simply because poetic theory does not always correspond to what poets actually write. It has also been true that the aesthetic principles for the haiku are often applied to other genres of Japanese art, such as *noh* play, flower arrangement, and the tea ceremony.

One of the most delicate principles of Eastern art is *yugen*. Originally *yugen* in Japanese art was an element of style pervasive in the language of *noh*, mentioned earlier. In reference to the *Works* by Zeami, the author of many of the extant *noh* plays, Arthur Waley expounds this difficult term *yugen*:

> It is applied to the natural grace of a boy's movements, to the gentle restraint of a nobleman's speech and bearing. "When notes fall sweetly and flutter delicately to the ear," that is the *yūgen* of music. The symbol of *yūgen* is "a white bird with a flower in its beak." "To watch the sun sink behind a flower-clad hill, to wander on and on in a huge forest with no thought of return, to stand upon the shore and gaze after a boat that goes hid by far-off islands, to ponder on the journey of wild-geese seen and lost among the clouds"—such are the gates to *yūgen*.[8]

Such scenes convey a feeling of satisfaction and release as does the catharsis of a Greek play, but *yugen* differs from catharsis because it has little to do with the emotional stress caused by tragedy. *Yugen* functions in art as a means by which human beings can comprehend the course of nature. Although *yugen* seems allied with a sense of resignation, it has a far different effect on the human psyche. A certain type of *noh* play like *Takasago* celebrates the order of the universe ruled by heaven.

The mode of perception in the play may be compared to that of a pine tree with its evergreen needles, the predominant representation on the stage. The style of *yugen* can express either happiness or sorrow. Cherry blossoms, however beautiful they may be, must fade away; love between man and woman is inevitably followed by sorrow.

This mystery and inexplicability, which surrounds the order of the universe, had a strong appeal to a classic haiku poet like Basho. His "The Old Pond," as discussed earlier, shows that while the poet describes a natural phenomenon realistically, he conveys his instant perception that nature is infinitely deep and absolutely silent. Such attributes of nature are not ostensibly stated; they are hidden. The tranquillity of the old pond with which the poet was struck remained in the background. He did not write, "The rest is quiet"; instead, he wrote the third line of the verse to read, "The sound of the water." The concluding image was given as a contrast to the background enveloped in quiet. Basho's mode of expression is suggestive rather than descriptive, hidden and reserved rather than overt and demonstrative. *Yugen* has all the connotations of modesty, concealment, depth, and darkness. In Zen painting, woods and bays, as well as houses and boats, are hidden; hence, these objects suggest infinity and profundity. Detail and refinement, which would mean limitation and temporariness of life, destroy the sense of permanence and eternity.

Sabi, another frequently used term in Japanese poetics, implies that what is described is aged. Buddha's portrait hung in Zen temples, as the Chinese painter Lian K'ai's *Buddha Leaving the Mountains* suggests, exhibits the Buddha as an old man in contrast to the young figure typically shown in other temples.[9] Zen's Buddha looks emaciated, his environment barren: his body, his tattered clothes, the aged tree standing nearby, the pieces of dry wood strewn around, all indicate that they have passed the prime of their life and function. In this kind of portrait, the old man with the thin body is nearer to his soul as the old tree with its skin and leaves fallen is to the very origin and essence of nature.

Sabi is traditionally associated with loneliness. Aesthetically, however, this mode of sensibility is characteristic of grace rather than splendor; it suggests quiet beauty as opposed to robust beauty. Basho's oft-quoted "A Crow" best illustrates this principle:

> A crow
> Perched on a withered tree
> In the autumn evening.

(Blyth, History 2: xxix)

Loneliness suggested by a single crow on a branch of an old tree is reinforced by the elements of time indicated by nightfall and autumn. The picture is drawn with little detail and the overall mood is created by a simple, graceful description of fact. Furthermore, parts of the picture are delineated, by implication, in dark colors: the crow is black, the branch dark brown, the background dusky. The kind of beauty associated with the loneliness in Basho's poem is in marked contrast to the robust beauty depicted in a haiku by Mukai Kyorai (1651–1704), one of Basho's disciples:

> Hanamori ya
> Shiroki kashira wo
> Tsuki awase

> [The guardians
> Of the cherry blossoms
> Lay their white heads together.]

> (Blyth, *History* 2: vii)

The tradition of haiku established in the seventeenth century produced eminent poets like Buson and Issa in the eighteenth century, but the revolt against this tradition took place toward the end of the nineteenth century under the banner of a young poet, Masaoka Shiki (1867–1902). On the one hand, Basho's followers, instead of becoming innovators as was their master, resorted to an artificiality reminiscent of the comic *renga*. On the other hand, Issa, when he died, left no disciples. The Meiji restoration (1868) called for changes in all aspects of Japanese culture, and Shiki became a leader in the literary revolution. He launched an attack on the tradition by publishing his controversial essay "Criticism of Basho." In response to a haiku by Hattori Ransetsu (1654–1707), Basho's disciple, Shiki composed his own. Ransetsu's haiku had been written two centuries earlier:

> Ki-giku shira-giku
> Sono hoka-no na wa
> Naku-mogana

> [Yellow and white chrysanthemums:
> What other possible names?
> None can be thought of.]

To Ransetsu's poem, Shiki responded with this one:

Kigiku shira-giku
Hito moto wa aka mo
Aramahoshi[10]

[Yellow and white chrysanthemums:
But at least another one—
I want a red one.]

Shiki advised his followers that they compose haiku to please themselves. To Shiki, some of the conventional poems lack direct, spontaneous expressions: a traditional haiku poet in his or her adherence
to old rules of grammar and devices such as *kireji* (cutting word),
resorted to artificially twisting words and phrases.

A modernist challenge that Shiki gave the art of haiku, however,
was to keep intact such aesthetic principles as *yugen* and *sabi*. Classic
poets like Basho and Issa, who adhered to such principles, were also
devout Buddhists. By contrast, Shiki, while abiding by the aesthetic
principles, was regarded as an agnostic. His philosophy of life is dem-
onstrated in this haiku:

Aki-kaze ya
Ware-ni kami nashi
Hotoke nashi[11]

[The wind in autumn
As for me, there are no gods,
There are no Buddhas.]

Although his direct reference to the divinities of Japanese culture smacks
of a modernist style, the predominant image created by "the wind in
autumn," a conventional *kigo*, suggests a deep-seated sense of loneliness
and coldness. Shiki's mode of expression in this haiku is based on *sabi*.

Some well-known haiku poets in the twentieth century also preserve the sensibility of *sabi*. The predicament of a patient described in
this haiku by Ishida Hakyo (1913–69) arouses *sabi*:

Byo shitsu ni
Subako tsukuredo
Tsubame kozu[12]

[In the hospital room
I have built a nest box but
Swallows never appear.]

Not only do the first and third lines indicate facts of loneliness, but also the patient's will to live suggested by the second line evoke a poignant sensibility. To a modern poet like Hakyo, the twin problems of humanity are loneliness and boredom. He sees the same problems exist in nature, as this haiku by him illustrates:

> Ori no washi
> Sabishiku nareba
> Hautsu ka mo

> [The caged eagle;
> When lonely
> He flaps his wings.]

(Blyth, History 2: 347)

The feeling of *sabi* is also evoked by the private world of the poet, the situation others cannot envision, as this haiku by Nakamura Kusatao (1901–83), another modernist, shows:

> Ka no koe no
> Hisoka naru toki
> Kui ni keri[13]

> [At the faint voices
> Of the flying mosquitoes
> I felt my remorse.]

Closely related to *sabi* is a poetic sensibility called *wabi*. Traditionally, *wabi* has been defined in sharp antithesis to a folk or plebeian saying, "Hana yori dango" (Rice dumplings are preferred to flowers). Some poets are inspired by the sentiment that human beings desire beauty more than food, what is lacking in animals and other nonhuman beings. *Wabi* refers to the uniquely human perception of beauty stemmed from poverty. *Wabi* is often regarded as religious as the saying "Blessed are the poor" suggests, but the spiritual aspect of *wabi* is based on the aesthetic rather than the moral sensibility.

Rikyu, the famed artist of the tea ceremony, wrote that food that is enough to sustain the body and a roof that does not leak are sufficient for human life. For Basho, however, an empty stomach was necessary to create poetry. Among Basho's disciples, Rotsu (1649–1738), the beggar-poet, is well known for having come into Basho's legacy of *wabi*. This haiku by Rotsu best demonstrates his state of mind:

Toridomo mo
Neitte iru ka
Yogo no umi

[The water-birds too
Are asleep
On the lake of Yogo?]

(Blyth, History 2: viii–ix)

Rotsu portrays a scene with no sight or sound of birds on the desolate lake. The withered reeds rustle from time to time in the chilly wind. It is only Rotsu the beggar and artist who is awake and is able to capture the beauty of the lake.

The sensibilities of *yugen*, *sabi*, and *wabi* all derive from the ways in which Japanese poets have seen nature over the centuries. Although the philosophy of Zen, on which the aesthetics of a poet like Basho is based, shuns emotion and intellect altogether, haiku in its modernist development by such a poet as Shiki is often concerned with one's feeling and thought. If haiku expresses the poet's feeling, human subjectivity, that feeling must be aroused by nature.

CHAPTER 2

BASHO AND HAIKU POETICS

To explain Basho's art of haiku, Yone Noguchi, a noted bilingual poet and critic, once quoted "Furu Ike ya" (The Old Pond), perhaps the most frequently quoted haiku: "The old pond! / A frog leapt into— / List, the water sound!"[1] One may think a frog is an absurd poetic subject, but Basho focused his vision on a scene of desolation, an image of nature. The pond was perhaps situated on the premises of an ancient temple whose silence was suddenly broken by a frog plunging into the deep water. As Noguchi conceived the experience, Basho, a Zen Buddhist, was "supposed to awaken into enlightenment now when he heard the voice bursting out of voicelessness, and the conception that life and death were mere change of condition was deepened into faith" (*Selected English Writings* 2: 74). Basho was not suggesting that the tranquillity of the pond meant death or that the frog symbolized life. Basho here had the sensation of hearing the sound bursting out of soundlessness. A haiku is not a representation of goodness, truth, or beauty; there is nothing particularly good, true, or beautiful about a frog leaping into the water.

It seems as though Basho, in writing the poem, carried nature within him and brought himself to the deepest level of nature, where all sounds lapse into the world of silence and infinity. Though his vision is based on reality, it transcends time and space. What a Zen poet like Basho is showing is that one can do enough naturally, enjoy doing it, and achieve one's peace of mind. This fusion of humanity and nature is called spontaneity in Zen. The best haiku, because of their linguistic limitations, are inwardly extensive and outwardly infinite. A severe constraint imposed on one aspect of haiku must be balanced by a spontaneous, boundless freedom on the other.

Basho's haiku is not only an expression of sensation, but it is also a generalization and depersonalization of that sensation. This characteristic can be shown by one of Basho's lesser-known haiku:

>Hiya-hiya to
>Kabe wo fumaete
>Hiru-ne kana[2]
>
>[How cool it is!
>Putting the feet on the wall:
>An afternoon nap.]

Basho was interested in expressing how his feet, anyone's feet, would feel when placed on a cool wall in the house on a warm summer afternoon. His sensation suggests that any other person would also enjoy the experience. Basho did not want to convey any emotion, any thought, any beauty; there remained only poetry, only nature.

That the art of haiku comes from human beings' affinity with nature is best explained by Basho in his travelogue *Oi no Kobumi* (*Manuscript in My Knapsack*):

>One and the same thing runs through the waka of Saigyō, the renga of Sōgi, the paintings of Sesshū, the tea ceremony of Rikyū. What is common to all these arts is their following nature and making a friend of the four seasons. Nothing the artist sees but is flowers, nothing he thinks of but is the moon. When what a man sees is not flowers, he is no better than a barbarian. When what he thinks in his heart is not the moon, he belongs to the same species as the birds and beasts. I say, free yourselves from the barbarian, remove yourself from the birds and beasts; follow nature and return to nature![3]

Basho's admonition in the passage suggests that haiku is the creation of things that already exist in nature but requires the artistic sensibility of a poet. What Basho is seeking in haiku composition is not beauty as in *waka*, but significance that underlies such an image as a jumping frog, a barking dog, a chirping cicada, or a bird on a branch.

To elicit significance from an image, the haiku poet must verify its existence. The image is concrete: Basho always emphasizes the material, as against the so-called spiritual. For him, there is no abstract arguing, no general principles. Significance emerges from an image and its surroundings, as shown in Basho's oft-quoted "Kare-Eda ni" (On a Withered Branch):

Kare-eda ni
Karasu-no tomari-keri
Aki-no-kure

(Henderson 18)

[On a withered branch
A crow has been perching
Autumn evening.]

In such a haiku, two entirely different things are joined in sameness: spirit and matter, present and future, word and thing, meaning and sensation. The haiku describes a crow that perches on a withered branch of a tree, a moment of reality. The image of a crow is followed by the coming of an autumn nightfall, a feeling of future. The poet may be feeling lonely. Present and future, thing and feeling, humanity and nature, each defining the other, are united.

Basho's haiku thrives on the expression of a temporary enlightenment, in which the reader sees into life of things. Although critics often relate Basho's enlightenment to Zen philosophy, it is not a matter of life and death for the soul. It is focused on life and its moment, however temporary it may be. As "On a Withered Branch" shows, that moment of revelation is clinched by the larger context suggested by "Autumn evening," a seasonal reference. It is toward the end of a year and at the end of a day. A crow, a lone figure, is resting on a withered branch. All these images are affecting the feeling of the poet. Not only does Basho's haiku exhibit a poignant interaction between the subjective and the objective, but there also emerges a unity of feeling that permeates the poem.

As his prose works, such as *Oi no Kobumi* and *Oku no Hosomichi* (*Narrow Road to the Interior*), suggest, Basho created his haiku out of his own imagination and experience. But critics have pointed out his worldview was influenced by ancient philosophies and religions such as Confucianism, Buddhism, and Zen. "Confucianism," R. H. Blyth noted, "contributed a certain sobriety, reserve, lack of extravagance and hyperbole, brevity and pithiness, and a moral flavour that may sometimes be vaguely felt, but is never allowed to be separated, as it is in Wordsworth and Hakurakuten, from the poetry itself" (*Haiku* 71).[4]

Basho was well versed in *The Analects*, which consists of Confucius's maxims and parables that have to do more with human life than with the life of a religious figure such as Christ and Buddha. Confucian ethics may be defined as a code of honor by which the individual must live in society. It consists of four virtues written in Chinese characters: 仁 (humanity), 義 (justice), 忠 (loyalty), and 孝 (filial piety). Basho, who read *The Analects*, wrote many haiku that express Confucian virtues. Basho wrote such haiku as these:

> Tsuka mo ugoke
> Waga naku koe wa
> Aki no kaze

> [Shake, O grave!
> My wailing voice
>   Is the autumn wind.]

> Te ni toraba
> Kien namida zo atsuki
> Aki no shimo

> [Should I take it in my hand,
> It would disappear with my hot tears,
>   Like the frost of autumn.]

> Nadeshiko ni
> Kakaru namida ya
> Kusunoki no tsuyu

> [The dew of the camphor tree
> Falls in tears
>   On the pinks.]

(*Haiku* 82)

In the first haiku Basho expresses an affinity between his wailing voice and the autumn wind. The second haiku focuses on his tears for his dead mother; the tears are so hot that his mother's hair would disappear like autumn frost. The third haiku draws an analogy between the virtue of loyalty and the dew of the camphor tree. This haiku, R. H. Blyth notes, "refers to Kusunoki and his son Masatsura, when they parted, in 1336, before the father's defeat and suicide" (*Haiku* 82).

These haiku suggest that, for Basho, Confucian virtues are derived from human sentiments as well as from natural phenomena. "This simple Confucianism," Blyth observes, "developed into something deeper and wider, embracing all nature in its scope, without losing its human feeling" (*Haiku* 82–83). The following haiku also express Confucian thought:

Yagate shinu
Keshiki mo miezu
Semi no koe

[Nothing intimates
How soon they must die,—?
Crying cicadas.]

Ōkaze no
Ashita mo akashi
Tōgarashi

[The morning
After the gale too,
Peppers are red.]

Hatsu-yuki ya
Suisen no ha no
Tawamu made

[The first snow,
Just enough to bend
The leaves of the daffodils.]

(*Haiku* 83)

The Confucian worldview, reflected in Basho's haiku, is also echoed by Nakae Toju (1608–48), one of the greatest thinkers in Japanese history. Toju said, "Heaven and Earth and man appear to be different, but they are essentially one. This essence has no size, and the spirit of man and the infinite must be one" (*Haiku* 80).

The unity of humanity and nature is also stressed in the *Saikontan*, said to be written by Kojisei, a collection of 359 short passages and poems, which was widely known in the Ming Dynasty in China. One of the passages reads: "Water not disturbed by waves settles down of itself. A mirror not covered with dust is clear and bright. The mind should be like this. When what beclouds it passes away, its brightness appears. Happiness must not be sought for; when what disturbs passes away, happiness comes of itself" (*Haiku* 75). Not only does this epigram demonstrate an affinity that exists between humanity and nature, it suggests that ethics is sanctioned by fact of nature rather than by human subjectivity.

Another passage provides an illustration of the way in which the human mind learns from nature: "The song of birds, the voices of insects, are all means of conveying truth to the mind; in flowers and grasses we see messages of the Way. The scholar, pure and clear of mind, serene and open of heart, should find in everything what nourishes him" (*Haiku* 76). This maxim admonishes the reader against human subjectivity: the less subjective the mind is, the more objective it becomes. The mind buttressed by nature thus enables ethics to be established.

In a later passage Kojisei states, "If your heart is without stormy waves, everywhere are blue mountains and green trees. If our real nature is creative like nature itself, wherever we may be, we see that all things are free like sporting fishes and circling kites" (*Haiku* 79). The human mind, as Kojisei observes, is often influenced by excessive emotion like anger. Once the mind is overwhelmed by such emotion and loses its control, it becomes alienated from ethics and universal truth. Kojisei's observation suggests that if human nature becomes destructive instead of creative like nature, it ceases to function.

Creation of ethics is possible, as Kojisei demonstrates, only if the mind is capable of seeing universal truth in nature. "The just man," Kojisei reasons, "has no mind to seek happiness; Heaven, therefore, because of this mindlessness, opens its inmost heart." On the other hand, he sees, "the bad man busies himself with avoiding misfortunes; Heaven therefore confounds him for this desire." Contrasting nature with humanity, he says, "How unsearchable are the ways of Heaven! How useless the wisdom of men!" (*Haiku* 75). What Kojisei calls "the ways of Heaven" are "unsearchable" and infinite; therefore, they constitute universal truth, the absolute values. Chapter 16 of *The Doctrine of the Mean*, a medieval Chinese text, quotes Confucius: "Confucius said, 'The power of spirits, how abundant! We look, but do not see them; we listen, but do not hear them; yet they sustain all things, and nothing is neglected by them'" (*Haiku* 73).

In Confucius's work, the universe consists of 天 (heaven), 地 (earth), and 人 (human). Some of the passages in *The Analects* express Confucius's thoughts and observations on the relationships among heaven, human, and God:

> How can a man conceal his nature? How can a man conceal his nature? (*Analects* 2. 10).
> He who offends against Heaven has none to whom he can pray (*Analects* 3. 12).
> He sacrificed to the spirits [God] as if the spirits were present (*Analects* 3. 12).

A virtuous man finds rest in his virtue (*Analects* 4. 2).

(*Haiku* 73)

For Confucius, God is not a living being like a human being: God is a concept that originates *from* a human being. The individual living in society thus formulates this concept by apprehending the ways of nature in heaven and on earth. God then reflects the conscience, a code of ethics established by the individual. Confucius sees that one who is endowed with ethics, "a virtuous man," is able to establish one's conscience. If a man is without virtues, on the other hand, he can neither conceal his nature nor rest peacefully in his life.

As Blyth has noted, "Confucianism is a much more poetical thing than most people suppose. In fact . . . one may say that what in it is poetical is true, using the word true in the sense of something that feeds the life of man, which can be absorbed into our own life and yet have a life of its own, which is organic and growing" (*Haiku* 71). In *Analects* 8.8, Confucius urges the reader to

> Arise with poetry;
> Stand with propriety;
> Grow with music.

(*Haiku* 72)

"The mind," Blyth remarks, "is roused by poetry, made steadfast by propriety, and perfected by music." *Analects* 9. 16 reads:, "Standing by a stream, Confucius said, 'It ceases not day or night, flowing on and on like this'" (*Haiku* 72). Not only is Confucius's description of the scene poetic and beautiful to look at, it conveys universal truth.[5]

Confucian thought is said to have inspired Japanese poets, including Basho. At the beginning of *The Analects*, Confucius says, "Is it not delightful to have a friend come from afar?" This saying, Blyth notes, inspired Basho to compose this haiku:

> Sabishisa wo
> Toute kurenu ka
> Kiri hito-ha

>   [A paulownia leaf has fallen;
> Will you not come to me
>   In my loneliness?]

(*Haiku* 71)

The haiku was addressed to his fellow haiku poet Ransetsu. Basho's wish to share his poetic vision with others suggests that one can model one's life after a code of ethics best defined in poetic words. That Confucius's advice "Stand with propriety" is mediated between the two actions "Arise with poetry" and "Grow with music" defines the meaning of the word *propriety*. This word in Confucius means, as Blyth explains, "a harmonious mode of living . . . a poetical way of doing everything . . . a deep, inward rightness of relation between ourselves and all outward circumstances" (*Haiku* 72). In Confucius, an individual must establish himself or herself by adhering to universal ethics. Once these ethics become the foundation of the individual, no other ideas and facts are to undermine that foundation.

As *The Analects* illustrates the ultimate truth, the fixed, immutable principles of the universe, some of Basho's haiku express the inevitability of whatever happens in human life, as well as the active acceptance of the inevitable. The following haiku by Basho depict the irreversible way of the universe to which a living being must conform:

> Ochizama ni
> Mizu koboshikeri
> Hanatsubaki

> [A flower of the camellia-tree
> Fell,
>   Spilling its water.]

(*Haiku* 10)

> Toshi kurenu
> Kasa kite waraji
> Hakinagara

> [The year draws to its close;
> But I am still wearing
>   My *kasa* and straw sandals.]

(*Haiku* 171)

"A Flower of the Camellia-Tree" describes the inevitability of natural phenomena: a flower fades as its water falls to the ground. "The Year Draws to Its Close," while describing the passing of a year, also suggests that even though the poet, wearing his hat and sandals, finds himself on the road, his journey must come to a close.

As Confucianism influenced Basho, so did Buddhism. He was a devout Buddhist all his life. Like Henry David Thoreau, an American transcendentalist who lived in close contact with nature, Basho traveled in the fields and the woods throughout his career. Both men were celibate; they were both fascinated with other living beings, animate or inanimate. That humans and nonhumans equally belong to the universe is a Confucian thought, and it is true of Buddhism. But, for Basho, there was a difference between Confucianism and Buddhism: Buddhism puts more emphasis on human compassion than does Confucianism. The doctrine that all things, even the inanimate, have the Buddha-nature distinguished Buddhism from Confucianism. Whereas Confucianism defines a cosmology, Buddhism is concerned with human nature. The reason for Thoreau's attraction to Buddhism rather than to Christianity was his realization that Buddhists believed in the existence of the soul in animals as Christians did not.[6]

Basho's stronger interest in others than in himself is best shown by this well-known haiku:

> Aki fuka ki
> Tonari wa nani wo
> Suru hito zo

> [It is deep autumn:
> My neighbor—
> How does he live, I wonder?]

(*Haiku* 158)

Feelings of unity and comradery, reflective of the Buddhistic philosophy, are motivated by a desire to perceive every instant in nature and humanity, an intuition that nothing is alone, nothing is out of the ordinary. This haiku creates a sense of unity and relatedness in society. Though a serious poet, Basho was enormously interested in the commonplace and the common people. In this haiku, as autumn approaches winter and perhaps he nears the end of his life, he takes a deeper interest in his fellow human beings. His observations of the season and his neighbor, a total stranger, are separate, yet both observations intensify each other. His vision, as it is unified, evokes a deeply felt, natural, and universal sentiment—compassion.

Just as human beings are united with compassion, there is also no clear-cut distinction between human and subhuman. "The polytheism of the ordinary Japanese, like that of the Greeks," Blyth observes, "had a great effect upon their mode of poetical life. The gods are many:

Amaterasu, Miroku, Hachiman, Jizō, Amida, Dainichi Nyorai, Tenjin, Kwannon, Emma O, Shakamuni, Benten, and a hundred others. . . . But these gods are not far from us, either in place or in rank. . . . The scale of beings in the Buddhist universe puts man midway. The primitive animistic ideas of the Japanese fall in with the Buddhist system, and all are united by the theory of transmigration" (*Haiku* 19). The following haiku by Basho illustrates that the soul exists in human beings as well as in nonhuman beings:

> Rusu no ma ni
> Aretaru kami no
> Ochiba kana
>
> [The god is absent;
> Dead leaves are piling,
>   And all is deserted.]

(*Haiku* 19)

In this haiku our sympathies are widened in both directions, toward gods as well as toward dead leaves.

Some of Basho's haiku express his sympathy with subhumans. His sympathy with animals may have derived from the theory of transmigration, but the following haiku suggests that his sympathy with the animate sprang spontaneously from his experience:

> Hatsu-shigure
> Saru mo komino wo
> Hoshige nari
>
> [First winter rain:
> The monkey also seems
>   To want a small straw cloak.]

(*Haiku* 297)

"Basho," Blyth notes, "was once returning from Ise, the home of the gods, to his native place of sad memories. Passing through the lonely forest, the cold rain pattering on the fallen leaves, he saw a small monkey sitting huddled on a bough, with that submissive pathos which human beings can hardly attain to. Animals alone possess it" (*Haiku* 297). In a similar vein Basho expresses human sympathy with another living being:

Takotsuboya
Hakanaki yume wo
Natsu no tsuki

[The octopuses in the jars:
Transient dreams
Under the summer noon.]

(*Haiku* 22)

The doctrine that all living things possess the Buddha-nature accounts not only for a religious sentiment but also for an innate human sensibility.

Not only was Basho inspired by Buddhism, especially by its doctrine of mercy, he was deeply influenced by Zen philosophy. Many of his haiku depict that one can do enough naturally and freely, enjoy doing it, and achieve one's peace of mind. This fusion of humanity and nature is called spontaneity in Zen. From a Zen point of view, such a vision is devoid of intellectualism and emotionalism. Since Zen is the most important philosophical tradition influencing Japanese haiku, as noted earlier, the haiku poet aims to understand the spirit of nature. Basho thus recognized little division between human and nature, man and woman, young and old; he was never concerned with the problems of good and evil.[7]

The most important concept that underlies Zen philosophy is the state of mind called *mu*, or nothingness. In *Nozarashi Kiko* (*A Travel Account of My Exposure in the Fields*), one of Basho's earlier books of essays, he opens with this revealing passage with two haiku:

When I set out on my journey of a thousand leagues I packed no provisions for the road. I clung to the staff of that pilgrim of old who, it is said, "entered the realm of nothingness under the moon after midnight." The voice of the wind sounded cold somehow as I left my tumbledown hut on the river in the eighth moon of the Year of the Rat, 1684.

Nozarashi wo	Bones exposed in a field—
Kokoro ni kaze no	At the thought, how the wind
Shimu mi ka na	Bites into my flesh.

Aki tō tose	Autumn? this makes ten years;
Kaette Edo wo	Now I really mean Edo
Sasu kokyō	When I speak of "home."

(Keene 81)

The first haiku conveys a sense of *wabi* because the image of his bones suggests poverty and eternity.[8] Although Basho endured fatigue and hardship on his journey, he reached a higher state of mind.[9] While he was aware of his physical and material poverty, his life was spiritually fulfilled. In this state of mind, having nothing meant having all.

For Basho, to enter the state of nothingness, one must annihilate oneself. The undisciplined self is often misguided by egotism. To live life freely, one must suppress subjectivity. Doho, Basho's disciple, wrote the following:

> When the Master said, "As for the pine, learn from the pine; as for the bamboo, learn from the bamboo," he meant cast aside personal desire or intention. Those who interpret this "learning" in their own way end up never learning.
>
> The phrase "learn" means to enter into the object, to be emotionally moved by the essence that emerges from that object, and for that movement to become verse. Even if one clearly expresses the object, if the emotion does not emerge from the object naturally, the object and the self will be divided, and that emotion will not achieve poetic truth [*makoto*]. The effect will be verbal artifice that results from personal desire. (Shirane 261)

Doho observed in Basho's haiku that the less subjective feeling is expressed, the more objective vision emerges. For example,

> Hara-naka ya
> Mono ni mo tsukazu
> Naku hibari
>
> [In the midst of the plain
> Sings the skylark,
> Free of all things.]

(*Haiku* 36)

> Niwa haite
> Yuki wo wasururu
> Hōki kana
>
> [Sweeping the garden,
> The snow is forgotten
> By the broom.]

(*Haiku* 36)

Yama mo niwa mo
Ugoki iruru ya
Natsuzashiki

[The mountains and garden also move;
The summer drawing room
    Includes them.]

(*Haiku* 38)

The first haiku, "In the Midst of the Plain," depicts the state of nothingness: the skylark, singing freely, is not singing of himself. The second haiku, "Sweeping the Garden," represents the primacy of nature
over humanity: the human activity is negated by a natural phenomenon. The third haiku, "The Mountains and Garden Also Move,"
exhibits the unity of nature and humanity: what appears to be a human
creation turns out to be part of nature.

Another aspect of the state of nothingness is loneliness. Basho
expresses human loneliness in such a haiku as this one:

Uki ware wo
Sabishi garaseyo
Kankodori

[Ah, *kankodori*,
Deepen thou
    My loneliness.]

(*Haiku* 161–62)

While Basho portrays his loneliness, he intimates that he is not alone
in nature. Even though the mountain bird's cry deepens his loneliness, it signifies that a living being is connected to another and that
nothing is isolated in nature. Basho's expression of loneliness is reminiscent of Langston Hughes's expression of the blues sensibility. In
"The Weary Blues," Hughes writes the following:

In a deep song voice with a melancholy tone
I heard that Negro sing, that old piano moan—
    "Ain't got nobody in all this world,
    Ain't got nobody but ma self.
    I's gwine to quit ma frownin'
    And put ma troubles on the shelf."

(*Selected Poems* 33)

Although the blues musician has no one with him, he keeps his soul intact with him. Like Basho, Hughes is portraying a state of isolation, loneliness, and poverty, which in turn enriches his soul.

The state of Zen, in which having nothing we possess all, implies paradox and contradiction. Rinzai (d. 867), a medieval Japanese Zen priest, was asked about the esoteric teaching of Dharma. He replied, "If there is any meaning in it, I myself am not saved." The interlocutor responded, "If it was meaningless, how was it the 2nd Patriarch (Eka) received the law?" Rinzai could only say, "This receiving is non-receiving" (*Haiku* 193). Basho's haiku "By Daylight," for instance, expresses such a paradox and contradiction:

> Hiru mireba
> Kubisuji akaki
> Hotaru kana

> [By daylight,
> The nape of the neck of the firefly
> Is red.]

(Haiku 200)

Basho was disillusioned, for in the dark the firefly emitted a golden light, but by daylight it looked merely red. This haiku is remindful of Emily Dickinson's poem "Success Is Counted Sweetest":

> To comprehend a nectar
> Requires sorest need.

For Dickinson, success in life is best appreciated by failure. Only those who fail can cherish those who succeed:

> As he defeated—dying—
> On whose forbidden ear
> The distant strains of triumph
> Burst agonized and clear!

(Complete Poems 35)

Just as the state of Zen yields an expression of paradox and contradiction, so does her view of success.

A Zen point of view enables one to see things in humanity and nature more objectively. Zen teaches us to gain freedom from our ideas and desires. Basho composed a haiku such as the following:

Kasa mo naki
Ware wo shigururu
Nanto nanto

[To be rained upon, in winter,
And not even an umbrella-hat,—
    Well, well!]

(*Haiku* 207)

From a human point of view, being rained on when you do not have
an umbrella is uncomfortable. From nature's perspective, however,
rain provides water for all objects in nature: water, nourishing plants
and animals, creates more life on earth. Such a haiku has an affinity
with Buson's haiku "An Autumn Eve":

Sabishisa no
Ureshiku mo ari
Aki no kure

[An autumn eve;
There is joy too,
    In loneliness.]

(*Haiku* 208)

From a human point of view, one might feel lonely in autumn, but from
nature's perspective, autumn is joyful. Basho's and Buson's haiku both
suggest that human beings are not alienated from nature. Another haiku
by Basho contrasts a human point of view with nature's perspective:

Michi-no-be no
Mokuge wa uma ni
Kuware keri

[The Rose of Sharon
By the roadside,
    Was eaten by the horse.]

(*Haiku* 217)

Basho was impressed with the beautiful rose of Sharon on the roadside, but the horse wanted to eat it. What he implies is something that
belongs to Zen: our desires and subjectivity are not always in harmony
with nature.

One of the salient techniques in Basho's haiku is a juxtaposition of images. In "The Old Pond," Basho made a stark contrast between the silence of the old pond and the sound of a jumping frog. In another famous haiku he also juxtaposed the silence that prevailed in the deep woods to the shrill voice of cicadas:

> Shizukesa ya
> Iwa ni shimiiru
> Semi no koe
>
> (*Haiku* 9)

> [How quiet it is!
> Piercing into the rocks
> The cicada's voice.]

Not only did Basho make a contrast between the opposing images, but he also juxtaposed the disparate ideas behind the images:

> meigetsu ya
> zani utsukushiki
> kao mo nashi
>
> (Shirane 103)

> [bright harvest moon—
> on the viewing stand
> not one beautiful face]

> Neko no koi
> Yamu toki neya no
> Oborozuki
>
> (*Haiku* 264)

> [The loves of the cats;
> When it was over, the hazy moon
> Over the bed-chamber.]

In "Bright Harvest Moon," Basho depicted the beautiful harvest moon. As he turned his eyes away from the moon to the earth, he did not even see one beautiful face among the moon viewers. Expressing his disillusionment, he was also suggesting the supremacy of nature over humanity. In "The Loves of the Cats," he initially focused on the loud, intense lovemaking of the cats. This image was juxtaposed to the quiet image of the hazy moon over his bedroom. As the collision of thoughts or images stimulates the poet, his mind is encouraged to make the effort to overcome the difficulty of uniting nature and humanity.

Basho is also known for the use of *kireji* (cutting word) in juxtaposing the images. The classic *renga* (linked song) had eighteen varieties of *kireji* for dividing its sections: *ya, kana, keri,* and so on. Basho increased the variety to forty-eight, as the use of *kireji* was refined and expanded. In "The Old Pond," mentioned earlier, *ya* is attached to the words *furu ike* (old pond): Basho is expressing a feeling of awe about the quietness of the pond. In "How Quiet It Is," Basho uses *ya* to emphasize the deadly quiet atmosphere of the woods he is visiting. Although "The Loves of the Cats" does not include a *kireji,* the first line is set off syntactically by the second line "Yamu toki" (When it was over). Above all, adding a *kireji* is a structural device to "cut" or divide a whole into parts. Since composing a haiku is confined to seventeen syllables in three lines, the parts of a vision or idea must be clearly segmented and united in their development. Dividing the whole into sections, in turn, gives the section with a *kireji* great weight. The use of cutting words thus signifies the poet's conviction about a natural phenomenon with which the poet is struck. Because the poet's response to the scene is interpreted as decisive, the overall vision created in the poem is further clarified. Traditionally, cutting words convey one's hope, wish, demand, call, question, resignation, awe, wonder, surprise, and the like.

Another technique that characterizes Basho's haiku is the unity of sentiments created in portraying nature and humanity. In the following haiku he unites the subjective with the objective, humanity with nature:

> araumi ya
> Sado ni yokotau
> amanogawa

> (Shirane 263)

> [a wild sea—
> stretching out to Sado Isle
> the Milky Way]

This haiku, describing a wild sea stretching out to Sado Island, a scene in nature Basho is watching, projects his own personal feeling.

Relating the poet's emotive state to a scene in nature is reminiscent of T. S. Eliot's objective correlative. Eliot's "The Love Song of J. Alfred Prufrock" begins with these three lines:

> Let us go then, you and I,
> When the evening is spread out against the sky
> Like a patient etherised upon a table.

> (*Complete Poems* 3)

Eliot is projecting the feeling of a patient on an operating table in a hospital to the evening spreading out against the sky. In Basho's and Eliot's verses, the scene in nature is unified with the feeling of the individual.

Basho also creates unity in expressing the senses. Basho's "Sunset on the Sea," for instance, shows the unity and relatedness of the senses:

> Umi kurete
> Kamo no koe
> Honoka ni shiroshi

> (Imoto 117)

> [Sunset on the sea:
> The voices of the ducks
> Are faintly white.]

The voices of the ducks under the darkened sky are delineated as white as well as faint. The chilled wind after dark evokes the whiteness associated with coldness. The voices of the ducks and the whiteness of the waves refer to two entirely different senses, but both senses, each reinforcing the other, create a unified sensation. In the following haiku, "Sinking into the Body" similarly unifies the senses of color and temperature:

> mi ni shimite
> daikon karashi
> aki no kaze

> (Shirane 95)

> [Sinking into the body
> The bitterness of the daikon
> The wind of autumn.]

The bitterness of the daikon, which depicts the senses of taste and color, is associated with the coldness of autumn wind. The association of the senses is, in turn, related to the poet's feeling, "Sinking into the Body."

In Basho's haiku, and indeed in classic haiku, the poet tries to relate human sentiments to nature. The use of *kigo* thus clarifies the poet's intention to unify the subjective with the objective, humanity and nature. The third line in "Sinking into the Body" constitutes a *kigo* referring to autumn. The close tie that haiku has to nature is manifested by making reference to one of the four seasons and appreciating its beauty or its significance. Conventionally, a letter in Japanese begins with a seasonal greeting and a reference to weather. This custom may have derived from the poets of the Muromachi period (1392–1573), who perceived the season in each climactic, environmental, and biological phenomenon—spring rain, autumn wind, winter snow, cherry blossoms, falling leaves, autumn sunset, the harvest moon—by which it became a literary representation. Seasonal words give each haiku vastness and universality it might not ordinarily have. This reference gives the poem a sense of infinity and eternity as it remains finite and temporary. In addition, the *kigo* serves an aesthetic function, since it has a capacity to evoke a commonly perceived image of beauty, as "the ducks," a *kigo* for summer, does in "Sunset on the Sea."

A seasonal reference in haiku functions as an objective correlative in relating the poet's sentiments to a phenomenon in nature. In associating the subjective with the objective, the poet focuses on an image in nature. The poet's aim is to depict the image that exists on its own object without reference to something other than itself.[10] As Ezra Pound observed, haiku is imagistic rather than symbolic. Whereas W. B. Yeats's symbolism was influenced by his cross-cultural visions of *noh* theater and Irish folklore, Pound's imagism had its origin in classic haiku.[11] In his essay "Vorticism," published in the *Fortnightly Review* in 1914, Pound defined the function of an image in haiku: an image is not a decorative emblem or symbol but a seed that germinates and develops into another organism. As an illustration he composed what he called "a hokku-like sentence": "The apparition of these faces in the crowd: / Petals, on a wet, black bough" ("Vorticism" 467).

Pound's use of images in this poem has an affinity with Basho's in such a haiku as "On a Withered Branch," discussed earlier: "On a withered branch / A crow has perched / Autumn evening." As the image of the faces in the crowd and the image of the petals on a wet bough interact with each other in Pound's poem, so do the image of a crow on a withered branch and the image of autumn evening in

Basho's haiku. Just as Pound actually saw these faces in the crowd, so did Basho see the crow momentarily resting on a branch. Each image made such a strong impression on the mind of the poet that the image transformed itself into another image. In Pound's poem the outward, objective image of the faces in the crowd "darts into a thing inward and subjective," the image of the petals on a wet, black bough ("Vorticism" 467). Whereas the faces in the crowd were real, the petals on a bough were imaginary. Similarly, the outward, objective image of a crow on a withered branch transformed into the image of autumn evening in Basho's mind. Pound called the image of the petals on a wet, black bough inward and subjective, for it was newly created in his mind. Although this image appeared imaginary, describing the petals with a wet and black bough evoked an outward and objective scene in late autumn or winter. Likewise, the image of autumn evening in Basho's haiku was created in the mind, but the description of the branch on which the crow perched as being withered made an inward, subjective image outward and objective.

Such a haiku as "On a Withered Branch" may be expressing the poet's feeling of loneliness, but this subjectivity is conveyed directly with a combination of objective images. The focus of Basho's vision is a lone crow. The branch the bird perches on is withered, the time is evening, and the season is autumn. These images, coalescing into a unified sensibility, suggest the emotive state of the poet. In Basho's haiku, nature exists as something real, concrete, and organic before his eyes, but at the same time nature, interacting with his mind, functions as a projection of his feelings. As a result, Basho's haiku is a simple, spontaneous expression of human sentiments. In the context of nature, Basho's expression of feelings becomes genuine, poignant, and free of any complicated or confused philosophical and social ideas.

CHAPTER 3

YONE NOGUCHI AND
JAPANESE POETICS

1

Yone Noguchi was born in a small town near Nagoya in 1875. In the late 1880s the young Noguchi, taking great interest in English texts used in a public school, read Samuel Smiles's writings on self-help. Perhaps inspired by Smiles, but in any case dissatisfied with his public school instruction, he withdrew from a middle school in Nagoya and went to Tokyo in 1890. At a prep school there he diligently read such Victorian writings as Thomas Macauley's, exactly the type of reading many a literary aspirant was doing on the other side of the Pacific.

A year later, detesting the national university an ambitious young man of his circumstance would be expected to attend, Noguchi entered Keio University, one of the oldest private colleges in Japan. There he studied Herbert Spencer and Thomas Carlyle, whose hero worship, in particular, made an impact on him. At the same time, he devoured such works as Washington Irving's *Sketch Book*, Oliver Goldsmith's "The Deserted Village," and Thomas Gray's "Elegy Written in a Country Churchyard." He even tried his hand at translating these eighteenth-century English poems into Japanese. On the other hand, he did not ignore his native culture. His lifelong interest in haiku and Zen dates from this period, and the frequent visits he made to Zen temples while in college established a practice he continued later in his career in Japan.[1]

Though two years of college provided him with omnivorous reading in English, the young aspiring poet was not content with his education, for he had been dreaming of living and writing in an English-speaking country. In the last decade of the nineteenth century, Japanese immigration to the United States was at a beginning stage, so it was not difficult for a young man without technical skills to obtain a passport and visa. His initial plans were to look for some sort of employment near San Francisco, where he arrived in December 1893 with little money in his pocket, and to continue his studies.

For the next two years, he lived mainly among the Japanese immigrants in California. For almost a year he was employed by a Japanese-language newspaper in San Francisco, and he spent a great deal of time translating news of the Sino-Japanese War sent from Japan. As a Japanese patriot he was delighted to learn about the triumphant military campaign in China. Once, however, his industry and interests led him to walk from San Francisco as far as to Palo Alto, where he was able to live for several months at a prep school near the campus of Stanford University and to read Edgar Allan Poe's poems.[2] His continued reading of *Sketch Book*, particularly Irving's portrayal of life in England, inspired him to travel someday across the Atlantic.

The turning point of Noguchi's life in America came in 1896, when twenty-one years old and already an aspiring poet in English, he paid homage to the Western poet Joaquin Miller. Miller in turn admired Noguchi's youth and enthusiasm. Except for a few occasions when Noguchi had to travel to Los Angeles partly on foot, or walk down the hills to see his publishers in San Francisco, he led a hermit's life for three years in Miller's mountain hut in Oakland. Through Miller, he became acquainted with Edwin Markham, Dr. Charles Warren Stoddard, and the publishers Gelett Burgess and Porter Garnett.

Within a year of meeting Miller, Noguchi published some of his earliest poems in three ephemeral journals of the day, *The Lark*, *The Chap Book*, and *The Philistine*. These poems attracted critical attention, and in the following year he brought out his first collections of poetry, *Seen and Unseen or, Monologues of a Homeless Snail*, and *The Voice of the Valley*. These, too, received praise. Willa Cather, for example, commenting on Yone Noguchi and Bliss Carman, the Canadian poet, wrote, "While Noguchi is by no means a great poet in the large, complicated modern sense of the word, he has more true inspiration, more melody from within than many a greater man" (Cather 2: 579). Despite initial success, however, his literary production became erratic, and his fragile reputation was not sustained for long. Like the traditional wandering bard in Japan, the young Noguchi spent his energy walking and reading in the high mountains and in the fields. Of this experience he wrote in his journal, "I thank the rain, the most gentle rain of the Californian May, that drove me into a barn at San Miguel for two days and made me study 'Hamlet' line after line; whatever I know about it today is from my reading in that haystack" (*Japan and America* preface).

Later, he traveled to Chicago, Boston, and New York, where, under the pseudonym Miss Morning Glory, he published a novella about a Japanese parlor maid.[3] After the turn of the century, he journeyed to England, where he published his third volume of poetry in English, *From the Eastern Sea*. This collection stirred some interest among the English readers, especially Thomas Hardy and George Meredith. "Your poems," Meredith wrote to Noguchi, "are another instance of the energy, mysteriousness, and poetical feeling of the Japanese, from whom we are receiving much instruction" (*Japan and America* 111).

Yone Noguchi's wandering journey came to an end when he returned to Japan in 1904, the year his son Isamu was born and left behind in America with the mother. The elder Noguchi became a professor of English at Keio University in Tokyo, the same college from which he had withdrawn eleven years earlier. Among the more than ninety books he wrote in Japan, many of them in English, four are genuine collections of English poetry.[4] The rest ranges from books of literary and art criticism to travelogues. In the midst of his burgeoning literary career in Japan, he sometimes came back to America and once visited England to deliver a lecture at Oxford's Magdalen College.

His role in East-West literary relations can scarcely be overestimated. The significance of his work should become even more evident when one tries to determine his influence on such major poets in Japan as Shimazaki Toson (1872–1943), Hagiwara Sakutaro (1886–1942), and Takamura Kotaro (1883–1956), as well as on W. B. Yeats, Ezra Pound, and Rabindranath Tagore, but most of all on the Imagist poets of the day.

The standard explanation for the influences of Japanese poetry, especially haiku, on T. E. Hulme and Ezra Pound is that they studied Japanese poetics through the Harvard sinologist Ernest Fenollosa, who had a poor command of the Japanese language. However, since Noguchi's later poetry collected in *The Pilgrimage* and his literary criticism, *The Spirit of Japanese Poetry* in particular, were widely circulated, the standard explanation seems questionable. (A detailed discussion of the influences Noguchi's writings might have had on Imagism will be given in Chapter 5.) Much more likely is the possibility that the Imagists responded directly to the example of their fellow poet Noguchi. Acknowledging the books Noguchi had sent him, Pound in London wrote a letter to Noguchi in Japan on September 2, 1911: "I had, of course, known of you, but I am much occupied with my mediaeval studies & had neglected to read your books altho' they lie with my own in Mathews shop & I am very familiar with the appearance of their covers. I am reading those you sent me but I do not yet know what to say of them except that they have delighted me. . . . You are giving us the spirit of Japan, is it not? very much as I am trying to deliver from obscurity certain forgotten odours of Provence & Tuscany." In response to Noguchi's earlier inquiries about Pound's views of art and criticism, Pound remarked: "Of your country I know almost nothing—surely if the east and the west are ever to understand each other that understanding must come slowly & come first through the arts. . . There is some criticism in the 'Spirit of Romance' & there will be some in the prefaces to the 'Guido' and the 'Arnaut.' But I might be more to the point if we who are artists should discuss the matters of technique & motive between ourselves." He added, "Also if you should write about these matters, I would discuss your letters with Mr. Yeats and likewise my answers. I have not answered before because your letter & your books have followed me through America, France, Italy, Germany and have reached me but lately. Let me thank you again for sending them, and believe me."[5]

In the 1920s and 1930s, Noguchi was also the most well-known interpreter of Japanese visual arts in the West, especially in England. Beginning with *The Spirit of Japanese Art*, he published in English ten volumes with colorful illustrations dealing with traditionally celebrated painters. Yeats, whose interest in the *noh* play is well known, wrote a letter to Noguchi in Japan from Oxford on June 27, 1921:[6] "Dear Noguchi: Though I have been so long in writing, your 'Hiroshige' has given me the greatest pleasure. I take more and more pleasure from oriental art; find more and more that it accords with what I aim at in my own work. . . . All your painters are simple, like the writers of Scottish ballads or the inventors of Irish stories, but one feels that Orpen and John have relatives in the patent office who are conscious of being at the fore-front of time." Greatly impressed by the Japanese paintings illustrated in Noguchi's books, Yeats commented on the relationships of art and life that underlie these paintings: "I would be simple myself but I do not know how. I am always turning over pages like those you have sent me, hoping that in my old age I may discover how. I wish somehow Japanese would tell us all about the lives . . . their talk, their loves, their religion, their friends . . . of these painters. . . . A form of beauty scarcely lasts a generation with us, but it lasts with you for centuries. You no more want to change it than a pious man wants to change the Lord's Prayer . . . not unless we have infected you with our egotism." Yeats closed his letter on a personal note: "I wish I had found my way to your country a year ago & were still there, for my own remains un[words blurred] as I dreaded that it would. I have not seen Galway for a long time now for I am warned that it is no place for wife and child" (Noguchi, *Collected English Letters* 220–21).

Noguchi's reputation as a poet and a critic grew in the West through the early 1930s, but World War II severed his ties to the West just as his relationship to his son Isamu had been strained ever since his birth. "I am getting old," Yone Noguchi wrote his son after the war, "and feel so sad and awful with what happened in Japan."[7] In 1947, in the midst of the chaos and devastation brought about by the war, without quite accomplishing his mission as he had wished, he died in Japan. Literary history, however, would amply justify that Yone Noguchi had played the most important role in modern times as a poet and interpreter of the divergent cultures of the East and the West.

2

Like his famous sculptor son, Isamu Noguchi, Yone Noguchi evolved his own distinct style, which drew on both Western and Eastern traditions. Noguchi's first book, *Seen and Unseen*, shows that he was initially inspired by Walt Whitman and Joaquin Miller. The affinity with nature, as reflected in these poems, is clearly derived from Japanese traditions, but the sweeping lines and his romanticized self, which abound in his poetry, are reminiscent of Whitman:

> The flat-boarded earth, nailed down at night,
>   rusting under the darkness:
> The Universe grows smaller,
>   palpitating against its destiny:
> My chilly soul—center of the world—gives seat
>   to audible tears—the songs of the cricket.
> I drink the darkness of a corner of the Universe,
>   . . .
> I am as a lost wind among the countless atoms
>   of high Heaven![8]

What unites the two men with different backgrounds is not only their style but their world vision. In "Song of Myself," Whitman includes under the name of Self body and soul, good and evil, man and woman. The conclusion of this section in the poem, where he introduces the concept of balance, is a lyrical passage that celebrates the ecstasy of love.

Whitman writes, "Prodigal, you have given me love—therefore I to you give love! / O unspeakable passionate love" (*Complete Poetry* 39). After this lyrical outburst, he declares, "I am not the poet of goodness only, I do not decline to be the poet of wickedness also . . . / I moisten the roots of all that has grown." As the poet of balance, Whitman accepts both good and evil; because he moistens the roots of all that has grown, he can call himself "a kosmos" (*Complete Poetry* 40–41). Noguchi's kosmos in "My Universe" has similar manifestations:

> The world is round; no-headed, no-footed,
>   having no left side, no right side!
> And to say *Goodness* is to say *Badness*:
> And to say *Badness* is to say *Goodness*.
> . . . .
> The greatest robber seems like saint:
> The cunning man seems like nothing-wanted beast!
> Who is the real man in the face of God?
> One who has fame not known,
> One who has Wisdom not applauded,
> One who has Goodness not respected:
> One who has n't loved Wisdom dearly,
> One who has n't hated Foolishness strongly!

> (*Selected English Writings* 1: 72–73)

Like Whitman, Noguchi believes in monism, and his ultimate goal in writing poetry is to achieve the ecstasies of the self in nature. Many of his early poems thus abound in the image in which life flows in on the self and others in nature. While Whitman in "Song of Myself" reincarnates himself into a sensitive quahog on the beach, Noguchi in "Seas of Loneliness" identifies himself with a lone quail:

> Underneath the void-colored shade of the trees,
>   my 'self' passed as a drowsy cloud into Somewhere.
> I see my soul floating upon the face of the deep,
>   nay the faceless face of the deepless deep—
> . . . .
> Alas, I, without wisdom, without foolishness,
>   without goodness, without badness,—am
>   like god, a negative god, at least!
> Is that a quail? One voice out of the back-hill
>   jumped into the ocean of loneliness

> (*Selected English Writings* 1: 67)

Though he became a different kind of nature poet after he returned to Japan, his later poems still bear out Whitman's influence. The last stanza of Noguchi's religious poem "By a Buddha Temple" reads,

> Ah, through the mountains and rivers,
>   Let thy vastness thrill like that of air;
> I read thy word in the flash of a leaf,
>   Thy mystery in the whisper of a grass.
>
> (*Selected English Writings* 1: 19)

Grass, which both poets love, is perhaps the most common and universal image in nature poetry. Such a technique, however, not only reveals the poet's sincere admiration of nature, but also betrays his abhorrence of civilization. In "Song of Myself," Whitman declares his independence from "civilization," which is represented by "houses and rooms." He detests the perfumes that envelop the domestic atmosphere because the fragrance is artificially distilled; the outdoor atmosphere, he argues, "is not a perfume, it has no taste of the distillation, it is odorless" (*Complete Poetry* 25). One of the disappointments Noguchi felt on his return to Japan was the rise of commercialism he witnessed. The beauty of the seashores near Tokyo was often marred by "the bathing crowd." But after summer, "with the autumn mellow and kind, the season of the clearest sky and softest breeze" (*Selected English Writings* 1: 19), he was able to recapture what Whitman called "Nature without check with original energy" (*Complete Poetry* 25):

> Into the homelessness of the sea I awoke:
>   Oh, my heart of the wind and spray!
> I am glad to be no-man to-day
>   With the laughter and dance of the sea-soul.[9]
>
> (*Selected English Writings* 1: 142)

Noguchi's aversion to people and to materialism in particular originated from his mentor Joaquin Miller, "the Poet of the Sierras," as he called him. It was Miller who urged the fledgling poet to live "amid the roses, quite high above the cities and people." Noguchi pays Miller this compliment: "Never did I think Miller was particularly eccentric, never even once during my long stay with him; he was the most natural man; and his picturesqueness certainly was not a crime" (*Selected English Writings* 2: 228). Once Miller brought him a bunch of poppies ("The golden poppy is God's gold" is Miller's song), say-ing that they were the state flower. Then, he recalls, Miller's lecture followed:

> The sweetest flowers grow closest to the ground; you must not measure Nature by its size: if there is any measure, it will be that of beauty; and where is beauty there is truth. First of all, you must know Nature by yourself, not through the book. It would be ten thousand times bet-ter to know by your own knowledge the colour, the perfume and the beauty of a single tiny creeping vine in the valley than to know all the Rocky Mountains through a book; books are nothing. Read the history written on the brows of stars! (*Selected English Writings* 2: 229).

Such an attitude as Miller inspired in him led to the art of poetry that Noguchi practiced in his early work. Remembering Miller's oft-repeated statement, "My life is like the life of a bird," he tried in "Alone in the Canyon" to relive the life of a creature, or merge him-self into the existence of a natural element:

> "Good-bye my beloved family"—I am to-night
>   buried under the sheeted coldness:
> The dark weights of loneliness make me immovable!
> Hark! the pine-wind blows,—blows!
> Lo, the feeble, obedient leaves flee down to the ground
>   fearing the stern-lipped wind voices!
> Alas, the crickets' flutes, to-night, are broken!
> The homeless snail climbing up the pillow,
>   stares upon the silvered star-tears on my eyes!
> The fish-like night-fogs flowering with mystery
>   on the Bare-limbed branches:—
>
>   (*Selected English Writings* 1: 67)

Far from being sentimentalized, a human being's harsh plight in nature is underscored by the images of coldness: the frozen ground, the blowing pine wind, the falling leaves, the crying crickets, the slowly climbing snail, the silvered stars above, the mysterious night fogs. This transformation of humanity into nature enables Noguchi in "To an Unknown Poet" to pose the following question: "When I am lost in the deep body of the mist on the hill, / The world seems built with me as its pillar! / Am I the god upon the face of the deep, deepless deepness in the Beginning?" (*Selected English Writings* 1: 61–62). In both poems Noguchi is speculating about the spiritual and transcendental power of humanity; conceptually, at least, he is uniting the will of a human being with the spirit of nature.

What Noguchi learned at the "Heights of the Sierras" was not only Miller's habit "to loaf and invite his own soul" in the presence of nature, a way of seeing nature, but also a way of experiencing love. For Noguchi, Miller was "the singer of 'a brother soul in some sweet bird, a sister spirit in a rose,' not the maker of loud-voiced ballads like the tide of a prairie fire or the marches of the Sierra mountains, but the dove-meek poet of love and humanity which . . . grow best and sweetest in silence." It is revealing that Noguchi's autobiography, written in Japan years later, reprints Miller's favorite poem on silence:

> Aye, Silence seems some maid at prayer,
> God's arm about her when she prays
> And where she prays and everywhere,
> On storm-strewn days or sundown days—
> What ill to Silence can befall
> Since Silence knows no ill at all?
> Vast silence seems some twilight sky
> That learns as with her weight of stars
> To rest, to rest, no more to roam,
> But rest and rest eternally.
> She loosens and lets down the bars,
> She brings the kind-eyed cattle home,
> She breathes the fragrant field of hay
> And heaven is not far away.
>
> (*Selected English Writings* 2: 232)

Many of Noguchi's poems, written both under the tutelage of Miller and later in Japan, echo Miller's ideas and methods of writing. In "My Poetry" (1897) Noguchi writes,

> My Poetry begins with the tireless songs of the cricket,
>   on the lean gray haired hill, in sober-faced evening.
> And the next page is Stillness—
> And what then, about the next to that?
> Alas, the god puts his universe-covering hand over its sheets!
> "*Master, take off your hand for the humble servant!*"
> Asked in vain:—
> How long for my meditation?
>
> (*Selected English Writings* 1: 65)

"Bird of Silence" (1909) deals with the same theme:

> Lonely ghost away from laughter and life,
> Wing down, I welcome thee,
> From the skies of thoughts and stars,
> Bird of Silence, mystery's brother, as white
> And aloof as is mystery,
> Tired of humanity and of voice,
> With thee, bird of Silence, I long to sail
> Beyond the seas where Time and sorrows die,
> . . . .
> I lost the voice as a willow spray
> To whom a thrill is its golden song,
> As a lotus whose break of cup
> Is the sudden cry after aerial dance.

(Selected English Writings 1: 22)

In this piece the poet is preoccupied with the idea of silence, because silence is "whole and perfect." Silence in nature provides humanity with rest and happiness, creating a sense of eternity. Through silence, the poet implies, you are able to establish "your true friendship with the ghosts and the beautiful. . . . You have to abandon yourself to the beautiful only to create the absolute beauty and grandeur that makes this our human world look trifling." Through imagination, then, you can achieve "true love, when the reality of the external world ceases to be a standard, and you yourself will be a revelation, therefore a great art itself, of hope and passion which will never fail."[10]

The theme of silence in Noguchi's poetry is furthermore related to that of death and eternity. In "Eternal Death" (1897), death is treated as if it were alive: "a thief . . . with long and dusty beard," "the poetry-planted garden of silence," "the pearl-fruited orchard of meditation," "the song of my heart strings." To Noguchi, life and death are but two phases of the human soul; death is as much "a triumph to me" as life (*Selected English Writings* 1: 71). "The real poetry," Noguchi once stated, "should be accidental and also absolute" (*Japan and America* 98). Such a poem as "Eternal Death" captures the exact circumstances where the natural phenomena reveal both meanings of the accidental and the absolute. His method is, indeed, akin to that of great Japanese poets who write only of isolated aspects of nature but sing mainly of infinity from their accidental revelation.

3

Although Noguchi owes his poetry to Whitman and Miller, one cannot overlook the Japanese poetics that underlies much of his work. The most obvious tie can be found in its subject matter. Just as Japanese haiku do not treat such subjects as physical love, sex, war, beasts, earthquakes, and floods, Noguchi's poems shun eroticism, ugliness, hate, evil, and untruth. Unlike some poets in the West, Japanese poets abhor sentimentalism, romance, and vulgarity. "The Japanese poetry," Noguchi cautions, "is that of the moon, stars, and flowers, that of a bird and waterfall for the noisiest" (*Spirit of Japanese Poetry* 18–19). Japanese poets' way of avoiding the negative aspects of life, such as illness, is best illustrated by the haiku Basho wrote at his deathbed:

> Lying ill on journey
> Ah, my dreams
> Run about the ruins of fields.[11]

(Selected English Writings 2: 70)

Japanese poetry is focused on nature because, as Noguchi says, "we human beings are not merely a part of Nature, but Nature itself" (*Selected English Writings* 2: 59). To be sure, this is pantheism; he is accepting humanity and nature as a whole and leaving them as they are. But more importantly he is suggesting that Japanese poets always go to nature to make human life meaningful, to make "humanity more intensive." They share an artistic susceptibility where, as Noguchi writes, "the sunlight falls on the laughter of woods and waters, where the birds sing by the flowers" (*Selected English Writings* 2: 68–69). This mystical affinity between humanity and nature, between the beauty of love and the beauty of natural phenomena, is best stated in this verse by Noguchi:

> It's accident to exist as a flower or a poet;
> A mere twist of evolution but from the same force:
> I see no form in them but only beauty in evidence;
> It's the single touch of their imagination to get the
>   embodiment of a poet or a flower:
> To be a poet is to be a flower,
> To be the dancer is to make the singer sing.[12]

(Selected English Writings 2: 69)

The fusion of humanity and nature, and the intensity of love and beauty with which it occurs, can be amply seen in haiku, as noted earlier. Noguchi regards Kikaku's haiku on the autumn moon as exemplary: "Autumn's full moon: / Lo, the shadows of a pine tree / Upon the mats!"[13] The beauty of the moonlight in Kikaku's haiku is not only humanized, since the moonlight shines on the human-made object, but also intensified by the shadows of an intricate pine tree on the mats. Noguchi himself unifies an image of humanity and that of nature in his own work. "Lines" (1909) begins with this verse:

> The sun I worship,
> Not for the light, but for the shadows of the trees he draws:
> Oh shadows welcome like an angel's bower,
> Where I build Summer-day dreams!
> Not for her love, but for the love's memory,

The poem ends on another suggestion of paradox:

> To a bird's song I listen,
> Not for the voice, but for the silence following after the song:
> O Silence fresh from the bosom of voice!—
> Melody from the Death-Land whither my face does ever turn!

> (*Selected English Writings* 1: 152)

As Kikaku unifies the images of the moonlight and the mats, Noguchi unifies those of the sun and the love, the bird and the poet. Through the paradox of union, both poets express the affinity of humanity and nature while at the same time maintaining an individual's separate identity and autonomy.

The most important tradition by which Noguchi's poetry is influenced is that of Zen. Zen practice calls for the austerity of the human mind; one should not allow his individuality to control his actions. "Drink tea when you are thirsty," says Noguchi, "eat food in your hunger. Rise with dawn, and sleep when the sun sets. But your trouble will begin when you let desire act freely; you have to soar above all personal desire" (*Story of Noguchi* 242). Zen does not recognize human reality, the existence of good and evil, because it is but the creation of one's will rather than the spirit of nature. The aim of the Zen poet, therefore, is to understand the spirit of nature. Observing the silent rites of a Zen priest, Noguchi once wrote, "Let the pine tree be green, and the roses red. We have to observe the mystery of every existence. . . . The language of silence cannot be understood by the way of reason, but by the power of impulse, which is abstraction" (*Story of Noguchi* 231–32).

To demonstrate the state of Zen, he composed a three-stanza poem, "By the Engakuji Temple: Moon Night," when he visited the Zen temple. The first two stanzas read,

> Through the breath of perfume,
> (O music of musics!)
> Down creeps the moon
> To fill my cup of song
> With memory's wine.
> Across the song of night and moon,
> (O perfume of perfumes!)
> My soul, as wind
> Whose heart's too full to sing,
> Only roams astray . . . [14]

(*Selected English Writings* 1: 136)

The poet's motivation for the union with nature, represented by the fragrance of the atmosphere and the moonlight, does not stem from his knowledge or desire. It is not the poet who is filling his "cup of song," but the moon that is creeping down. In the second stanza the poet reaches the state of Zen where, giving himself, he enters wholly into his actions—"the song of night and moon." That his soul is roaming astray suggests that he is giving up the ego. The loss of individuality within the union with nature is a condition of what R. H. Blyth calls, as noted earlier, "absolute spiritual poverty in which, having nothing, we possess all" (*Haiku* 162).

In haiku, there is little division between the perceiver and the perceived, spirit and matter, humanity and nature. "In the realm of poetry," Noguchi maintains, "there is no strict boundary between the domains generally called subjective and objective; while some *Hokku* poems appear to be objective, those poems are again by turns quite subjective through the great virtue of the writers having the fullest identification with the matter written on" (*Selected English Writings* 2: 73). Noguchi's poem "The Passing of Summer" (1909) reads,

> An empty cup whence the light of passion is drunk!—
> To-day a sad rumour passes through the trees,
> A chill wind is borne by the stream,
> The waves shiver in pain;
> Where now the cicada's song long and hot?

(*Selected English Writings* 1: 149)

Such phrases as "the light of passion" and "the cicada's song long and hot" are not metonymies of summer; they directly depict the summer. In Noguchi's poetry, as in traditional haiku, poetry and sensation are spontaneously joined, so that there is scarcely any room left for human subjectivity.

Not all of Noguchi's English poems adhere to Japanese traditions. Most of his early poems, collected in *Seen and Unseen* and *The Voice of the Valley*, are beautiful expressions of the young poet's delight in his dreams, reveries, and mysteries about nature and the high Sierras, where he actually spent his life as a recluse. But the relationship of humanity to nature that he creates in his early work is quite different from that of his later work. The ecstasies of the self in nature described in his early poetry are sometimes overindulgent, and this dependency of the self on nature results in a loss of equilibrium between them. Speaking of the same experience, Whitman cautions his own senses: "You villain touch! . . . / Unclench your floodgates, you are too much for me" (*Complete Poetry* 46). Unlike Whitman, however, the young Noguchi is at times unable to resist an urge toward overstatement and crude symbolism. In his poem "In the Valley," for example, the reveries of nature are most appropriately represented in terms of "the Sierra-rock, a tavern for the clouds" and "the Genii in the Valley-cavern." Man's will and desire, on the other hand, are alluded to by such prosaic expressions as "Fame" and "Gold"; "Heaven" and "mortals" are merely equated with "Glory" and "Decay" (*Selected English Writings* 1: 81–82).

Such a poem as "In the Valley" smacks of didacticism and moralism. It is not these qualities in his early poetry that attracted critics' attention. It is, to use his editor's phrase, "this unconventional child of nature . . . whose heart and soul lie naked and bare. . . . If he is sometimes obscure, it is because he had flown into cloud-land, where obscurity is a virtue."[15] Noguchi himself believed in the virtue of obscurity and indefiniteness in poetry and in art. To show this characteristic, he quotes the English translation of a haiku found in an anthology:

> "Thought I, the fallen flowers
> Are returning to their branch
> But lo! they are butterflies."

Noguchi can only say that if this poem "means anything, it is the writer's ingenuity perhaps in finding a simile; but I wonder where is its poetical charm when it is expressed thus definitely" (*Selected English Writings* 2: 115–16).

What Noguchi strove to accomplish in his poetry, particularly in his later career, was to perceive a harmonious relationship between humanity and nature. For him, the aim of poetry is not only to achieve the union of humankind and nature, but also to maintain the identity of each within that union. The poet's chief function is not to express the feelings of human beings by the spirits of nature. This is analogous to what Noguchi saw in the print *Autumnal Moon at Tamagawa* by Hiroshige, an eminent nineteenth-century Japanese landscape painter, in which the moon over the river, the low mountain ranges in the background, and the fishermen engaged in night work are all harmoniously blended into a whole picture. Hiroshige in this painting, as Noguchi realizes, is not attempting to imitate nature or to make a copy whereby "the artist may become a soft-voiced servant to nature . . . not a real lover who truly understands her inner soul" (*Selected English Writings* 2: 184). In providing expression for nature, the artist must not express his own thought and logic. When Wordsworth sings, "I wandered, lonely as a cloud," he is simply feeling akin to the cloud, rather than imposing the human will on the will of nature. Similarly, in Noguchi's successful poems, humans' position in nature becomes neither subordinate nor obtrusive, and both worlds can maintain a sense of dignity and autonomy.

CHAPTER 4

W. B. YEATS'S POETICS
IN THE *NOH* PLAY

Since childhood, Yeats felt in his heart that "only ancient things and the stuff of dreams were beautiful" (*Reveries* 82). It was the rise of science and realism in the Victorian age that directed his attention to the Middle Ages and the world of myths and legends. As he read *Certain Noble Plays of Japan*, translated by Ezra Pound and Ernest Fenollosa in 1916, he found in them what he would emulate in reshaping his own poetic drama. "In fact," he wrote, "with the help of these plays . . . I have invented a form of drama, distinguished, indirect and symbolic, and having no need of mob or press to pay its way—an aristocratic form" (*Classic Noh Theatre* 151). Initially he was attracted to *noh*, which had developed from religious rites practiced in the festivals of the Shinto gods, as Fenollosa notes in *The Classic Noh Theatre of Japan*. Although there is no controversy over who introduced Yeats to the *noh* play, critics have overlooked other sources on which he might have relied.[1]

Having lived many years in Japan as an art historian, Fenollosa became well versed in Japanese art and literature, but his actual knowledge of the language was not profound.[2] Pound, on the other hand, who edited Fenollosa's notes, had no knowledge of Japanese, either. Since he did not visit Japan, he was unable to see the actual performance of a *noh* play in Japanese. Nor did he have firsthand knowledge of the drama and its cultural background. The most likely source of information available to Yeats, besides Fenollosa and Pound, was Yone Noguchi, who had by the mid-1910s published not only such widely read books of criticism in England and America as *The Spirit of Japanese*

Poetry (1914) and *The Spirit of Japanese Art* (1915), as noted earlier, but also several collections of his own poems in English.[3] In *The Spirit of Japanese Poetry*, in particular, Noguchi included a long discussion of *noh* titled "No: The Japanese Play of Silence" with his own composition of a *noh* play in English, "The Morning-Glory: A Dramatic Fragment" (54–70). Noguchi was also invited to contribute another English *noh* play, "The Everlasting Sorrow: A Japanese Noh Play" (1917), and an article, "The Japanese Noh Play" (1918), to *The Egoist*.[4]

1

Not only through Noguchi's writings did Yeats learn about Japanese art and literature, and the *noh* play in particular, but he also made much of his acquaintance with Noguchi in person. Noguchi, in fact, delivered in England several lectures on Japanese art and literature. Among them, "The Japanese *Hokku* Poetry" was a lecture given at Oxford's Magdalen College in January 1914 at the invitation of Robert Bridges, the poet laureate, and Dr. T. H. Warren, president of the college.[5] In the same month Noguchi gave another lecture, "Japanese Poetry" at the Japan Society of London.[6] It seems as though Yeats's interest in Japanese painting and *noh* coincided with the publication of Noguchi's essays and lectures on these subjects during this period.

But Yeats's personal acquaintance with Noguchi goes back to a decade earlier. Yeats first met Noguchi in 1903. Many years later Yeats wrote, in part, to Noguchi, who was in Japan,

> When a Japanese, or Mogul, or Chinese painter seems to say, "Have I not drawn a beautiful scene," one agrees at once, but when a modern European painter says so one does not agree so quickly, if at all. . . . The old French poets were simple as the modern are not, & I find in Francois Villon the same thoughts, with more intellectual power, that I find in the Gaelic poet [Raftery]. I would be simple myself but I do not know how. I am always turning over pages like those you have sent me, hoping that in my old age I may discover how. (*Collected English Letters* 220–21)

As this letter suggests, Yeats's introduction to the *noh* came after his fascination with the oriental paintings he had seen in England. His interest in Japanese visual arts was intensified by Noguchi's *The Spirit of Japanese Art* (1915) and later by his *Hiroshige* (1921), which was produced with numerous collotype illustrations and a colored frontispiece.[7] What seemed to have inspired Yeats was the "simplicity" of the artists, a century-old form of beauty that transcends time and place. Irked by modern ingenuity and science, he was adamantly opposed to realism in art and literature. For him, realism failed to uncover the deeply ingrained human spirit and character. He later discovered that noble spirits and profound emotions are expressed with simplicity in the *noh* play. His statement about the simple beauty of Japanese arts echoes what Noguchi characterizes the *noh* drama. "It was the time," Noguchi writes, "when nobody asked who wrote them, if the plays themselves were worthy. What a difference from this day of advertisement and personal ambition! . . . I mean that they are not the creation of one time or one age; it is not far wrong to say that they wrote themselves, as if flowers or trees rising from the rich soil of tradition and Buddhistic faith" (*Spirit of Japanese Poetry* 63).

Yeats and Noguchi thus shared the notion that simplicity and naturalness in Japanese arts came from the cultural backgrounds of the arts rather than the personal emotions of artists. Yeats clearly implied in his letter to Noguchi that contemporary arts in the West were "infected with egotism," while classical works of art in Japan, as Noguchi observed, were created as if anonymously. "The names of the authors, alas," Noguchi writes, "are forgotten, or they hid their own names by choice. Even when some of their names, Seami [Zeami] and Otoami for instance, are given, it is said by an authority that they are, in fact, only responsible for the music, the dance, and the general stage management" (*Spirit of Japanese Poetry* 63).

Among the classic arts in Japan, the *noh* drama had the strongest appeal to Yeats because it was buttressed by a spiritual and philosophical foundation. Although Yeats was introduced to *noh* through Fenollosa's historical accounts of the genre, first published in 1916, he might have acquired further knowledge from Noguchi's *The Spirit of Japanese Poetry* (1914). In it Noguchi reminds the reader that as the Japanese tea ceremony grew out of Zen, the *noh* drama had an intimate connection with Buddhism. Among the three hundred existing *noh* plays, he points out, there is no play in which a priest does not appear to offer prayers so that the ghost of a warrior, a lady, a flower, or a tree may attain Nirvana. The purpose of a *noh* play is to recount "the human tragedy rather than comedy of the old stories and legends seen through the Buddhistic flash of understanding" (63). To Yeats, such a form of beauty as seen in the classic art of Japan, which lasts for centuries, changes no more than the Lord's Prayer or the crucifix on the wall portrayed in the classic art of Europe does.

The spiritual foundation of the *noh* drama also has a corollary to the abhorrence both Yeats and Noguchi felt about realism and sensationalism in contemporary arts. In place of surface realism, a great dramatist would employ rituals and masks. When Yeats was introduced to the *noh* theater, he was at once impressed with such devices. In the performance of *At the Hawk's Well*, he used masks to present intensified, time-honored expressions as the Roman theater "abandoned 'make-up' and used the mask instead." He thought the use of the mask is "to create once more heroic or groteque types that, keeping always an appropriate distance from life," would seem to be images of "those profound emotions that exist only in solitude and in silence" rather than in actual scenes and personages (*Plays of Yeats* 416). His idea about the mask, in fact, repeats Noguchi's: "the mask," Noguchi argues, "is made to reserve its feeling, and the actors wonderfully well protect themselves from falling into the bathos of the so-called realism through the virtue of poetry and prayer" (*Spirit of Japanese Poetry* 60).

The comments Yeats made after the performance of *At the Hawk's Well* in 1917 are foreshadowed in a passage written in the previous year:

> A mask never seems but a dirty face, and no matter how close you go is still a work of art; nor shall we lose by staying the movement of the features, for deep feeling is expressed by a movement of the whole body. In poetical painting and in sculpture the face seems the nobler for lacking curiosity, alert attention, all that we sum up under the famous word of the realists "vitality." It is even possible that being is only possessed completely by the dead, and that it is some knowledge of this that makes us gaze with so much emotion upon the face of the Sphinx or Buddha. . . . Let us press the popular arts on to a more complete realism, for that would be their honesty; and the commercial arts demoralise by their compromise, their incompleteness, their idealism without sincerity or elegance, their pretence that ignorance can found a true theatre of beauty. (*Classic Noh Theatre* 155–56)

In *The Spirit of Japanese Poetry*, published a few years earlier than Yeats's essay, Noguchi, as if to call for Yeats's response, had written,

> When the Japanese poetry joined its hand with the stage, we have the *No* drama, in which the characters sway in music, soft but vivid, as if a web in the air of perfume; we Japanese find our joy and sorrow in it. Oh, what a tragedy and beauty in the *No* stage! I always think it would be certainly a great thing if the *No* drama could be properly introduced into the West; the result would be no small protest against the Western stage, it would mean a real revelation for those people who are well tired of their own plays with a certain pantomimic spirit underneath. (*Spirit of Japanese Poetry* 11)

2

The salient feature of *noh* that must have held a strong appeal for Yeats is the structure of a *noh* play. Unlike a realistic, mimetic play in the West, the *noh* play thrives on its unity and concentration. It was Pound again who called Yeats's attention to this play as a concentrated image. In "Vorticism," an essay on imagism published in *The Fortnightly Review* in 1914, Pound included this note: "I am often asked whether there can be a long imagiste or vorticist poem. The Japanese, who evolved the hokku, evolved also the Noh plays. In the best 'Noh' the whole play may consist of one image. I mean it is gathered about one image. Its unity consists in one image, enforced by movement and music" (471). Pound's statement, however, was derived from Fenollosa, who wrote: "The beauty and power of Noh lie in the concentration. All elements—costume, motion, verse, and music—unite to produce a single clarified impression. Each drama embodies some primary human relation or emotion; and the poetic sweetness or poignancy of this is carried to its highest degree by carefully excluding all such obtrusive elements as a mimetic realism or vulgar sensation might demand. The emotion is always fixed upon idea, not upon personality" (*Classic Noh Theatre* 69).

Fenollosa's notes, moreover, made Pound realize that a series of different *noh* plays presents "a complete service of life" (11). Visions of life portrayed on the *noh* stage are not segmented; they are continuous and unified. "We do not find," Pound reminds the reader, "as we find in Hamlet, a certain situation or problem set out and analyzed. The Noh service presents, or symbolizes a complete diagram of life and recurrence" (11–12). In some ways *noh* resembles the Greek play, for the individual plays deal with well-known legends and myths. As an Oedipus play treats the character of Oedipus in a known predicament, *Suma Genji*, for example, features Shite, an old woodcutter, who appears as the ghost of the hero Genji at the seashore of Suma.

To present a cycle of life and death, the *noh* play often employs spirits and ghosts. Such a structural device, obviously different from the Western convention of plot, accounts for the different philosophy of life that underlies *noh*. As if to explain this difference, Noguchi made a modest proposal for Western writers. "I think," he urged, "it is time for them to live more of the passive side of Life and Nature, so as to make the meaning of the whole of them perfect and clear, to value the beauty of inaction so as to emphasize action, to think of Death so as to make Life more attractive" (*Spirit of Japanese Poetry* 24). The concept of unity and continuity expressed in Japanese literature primarily stemmed from Zen Buddhism, which teaches its believers to transcend the dualism of life and death. Zen master Dogen (1200–54), whose work *Shobogenzo* is known in Japan for his practical application rather than his theory of Zen doctrine, said that because life and death are beyond human control, there is no need to avoid them (Kurebayashi 121–29). Dogen's teaching is a refutation of the assumption that life and death are entirely separate entities as are seasons.

Among the fifteen *noh* plays translated by Fenollosa and Pound, seven of them present characters that appear as spirits and ghosts to interact with living persons. In *Nishikigi* the priest has a dream in which the unrequited love of a dead man for a living woman is consummated through the priest's prayer. Yeats's *The Dreaming of the Bones* (1919) has a plot structure strikingly similar to that of *Nishikigi*: the lovers Diarmuid and Dervorgilla as spirits brought the Norman invaders into Ireland after seven centuries to consummate their love by an Irish revolutionary taking the role of a *noh* priest. The image of man and spirit recurs frequently in Yeats's later poem, "Byzantium" (1930):

> Before me floats an image, man or shade,
> Shade more than man, more image than a shade;

Yeats's attempt to reconcile life and death also extends to other opposites in human life—body and soul, man and spirit:

> A mouth that has no moisture and no breath
> Breathless mouths may summon;
> I hail the superhuman;
> I call it death-in-life and life-in-death.

> (*Poems of Yeats* 248)

There is nothing new in the West, however, about the poet's bringing the rich opposites into a unified vision. Whitman seeks a reconciliation between life and death, man and God, and other oppositions. He turns the bereavement in "When Lilacs Last in the Dooryard Bloom'd" into a celebration of death. In "A Sight in Camp in the Daybreak Gray and Dim," the poet, after seeing two of his comrades lying dead, one old and another young, comes upon a third—"a face nor child nor old, very calm, as of beautiful yellow white ivory." The third dead soldier is identified with "the Christ himself, / Dead and divine and brother of all, and here again he lies" (*Leaves of Grass* 2: 496). But the problem with Western poetry and drama, Yeats felt, was the lack of intensity and artistry in presenting the image of unity and continuity.

One of the disagreements between Pound and Yeats was that Pound regarded symbolism as "a sort of allusion, almost of allegory." The symbolists, Pound thought, "degraded the symbol to the status of a word. . . . Moreover, one does not want to be called a symbolist, because symbolism has usually been associated with mushy technique" ("Vorticism" 463). For Pound, symbolism is inferior to imagism because in symbolism one image is used to suggest another or to represent another, whereby both images would be weakened. His theory of imagism was derived from haiku, which traditionally shuns metaphor and symbolism, rather than from the *noh* play, which Yeats considered "indirect and symbolic." If Yeats's ideal language has the suggestiveness and allusiveness of symbolism as opposed to the directness and clearness of imagism, then his sources certainly did not include Pound. Even though Yeats dedicated *At the Hawk's Well* to Pound, Yeats was not enthusiastic for Pound's theory. "My own theory of poetical or legendary drama," Yeats wrote to Fiona Macleod, "is that it should have no realistic, or elaborate, but only a symbolic and decorative setting. A forest, for instance, should be represented by a forest pattern and not by a forest painting" (Sharp 280–81). In short, Yeats, a symbolist and spiritualist poet, was fascinated by the *noh* play, while Pound, an Imagist, was influenced by Japanese poetry and by haiku in particular.

For this technique of symbolism on the *noh* stage, the notes by Pound and Fenollosa were of great use to Yeats, who was eager to adapt an image that unifies the play or an action that foreshadows the outcome. The well in *At the Hawk's Well*, the birds in *Calvary*, and Cuchulain lying on his deathbed in *The Only Jealousy of Emer* were all consciously modeled on the *noh* play. In 1920 Arthur Waley, who translated with success the monumental *Tale of Genji*, also published *The Nō Plays of Japan*, a translation of over twenty well-known plays with lengthy notes, but his writings were of no particular interest to Yeats. Waley's introduction is primarily a historical survey of the genre with well-detailed biographical and textual notes on Zeami, the most celebrated *noh* dramatist. The only native scholar writing in English was Yone Noguchi, who not only wrote about *noh* but also tried his hand at composing *noh* plays in English.

Yeats's interest in the symbolism used on the *noh* stage came from a desire to condense and simplify the action of his plays. This means that action must be reduced to its essentials and that the characters involved in it must be freed from anything that may distract the viewer's attention from the meaning of the play. The stage does not show any elaborate scenery, nor do subsidiary persons appear on the scene. The stage for the well-known *Takasago*, for instance, contains an old painted pine tree, which, Noguchi describes, "looms as if a symbol of eternity out of the mist." The word *pine-tree*, signifying "the hosts of pine-trees in the shapes of an old man and woman singing deathlessness and peace," is repeated throughout the performance. On the gallery connected with the stage, Noguchi says, "*No* actors move as spectres and make the performance complete, the passage of a beginning and ending, I might say Life and Death" (*Spirit of Japanese Poetry* 58).

Simplicity and concentration are so essential to the performance of a *noh* play that the stage itself must be physically small and confined. "There is no other stage like this *No* stage," Noguchi emphasizes. "The actors and audience go straight into the heart of prayer in creating the most intense atmosphere of grayness, the most suggestive colour in all Japanese art, which is the twilight soared out of time and place." As Yeats would wholeheartedly have agreed, "It is a divine sanctuary where the vexation of the outer world and the realism of modern life" are left behind (*Spirit of Japanese Poetry* 55–58). Anything that gets in the way of concentration, such as scenery, is eliminated. In the notes to *At the Hawk's Well*, Yeats writes,

> I do not think of my discovery as mere economy, for it has been a great gain to get rid of scenery, to substitute for a crude landscape painted upon canvas three performers who, sitting before the wall or a patterned screen, describe landscape or event, and accompany movement with drum and gong, or deepen the emotion of the words with zither or flute. Painted scenery, after all, is unnecessary to my friends and to myself, for our imagination kept living by the arts can imagine a mountain covered with thorn-trees in a drawing-room without any trouble, and we have many quarrels with even good scene-painting. (*Plays of Yeats* 415–16)

Equally effective is the use of the mask that enables the actors and audience alike to concentrate on the meaning of the play. "*No*," as Noguchi reminds the English reader, "is the mask play to speak directly . . . which, marvellously enough, seems to differentiate the most delicate shades of human sensibility; we should thank our own imagination which turns the mood to a spirit more alive than you or I, when neither the actors nor the mask-carvers can satisfactorily express their secret" (*Spirit of Japanese Poetry* 59–60). The mask, a permanent work of art, is made to preserve its feeling so that the actors, uninfluenced by the superficial actuality, protect themselves from falling into what Noguchi calls "the bathos of reality which would, in nine cases out of ten, alienate them from the rhythmical creation of beauty" ("Japanese Noh Play" 99). Yeats was convinced of the notion that the mask can convey legendary emotions far more artistically than the actual face of an actor. For his Cuchulain, a legendary figure, can show with the mask "a face, not made before the looking-glass by some leading player . . . but moulded by some distinguished artist." For Yeats, the device of the mask is a culmination of the joint effort by a poet and an artist to keep "an appropriate distance from life" (*Plays of Yeats* 416).

Another structural device is the dance performed at the climax. Dance in *noh* is not choreographic movement as in the ballet, but, as Yeats cautions, "a series of positions and movements which may represent a battle, or a marriage, or the pain of a ghost in the Buddhist purgatory." While the Western dance often presents mimetic movements of arms or body to express physical beauty, dancers in *noh*, always keeping the upper part of their body still, "associate with every gesture or pose some definite thought." The focus of attention in the *noh* dance is not on the human form, but on the rhythm to which it moves. "The triumph of their art," Yeats recognizes, "is to express the rhythm in its intensity." The aim of such dance is to intensify the deep meaning of the play, and the deeper the meaning is, the fewer and simpler the gesture of the dance. As Yeats observed, dances in the *noh* stage "pause at moments of muscular tension." The dancers walk on the stage "with a sliding movement, and one gets the impression not of undulation but of continuous straight lines" (*Classic Noh Theatre* 158).

The function of dance in *noh* was later adapted to Yeats's poetry. In "Among School Children," for example, Yeats uses the metaphor of the dance to suggest a unity of oppositions in human life:

> Labour in blossoming or dancing where
> The body is not bruised to pleasure soul,

In Yeats's vision the body and the soul become indistinguishable because of the unifying image of the dance:

> O chestnut tree, great rooted blossomer,
> Are you the leaf, the blossom or the bole?
> O body swayed to music, O brightening glance,
> How can we know the dancer from the dance?

> (*Poems of Yeats* 217)

In a similar vein, Noguchi as a Japanese poet goes to nature to make life more meaningful; he, too, tries to bring the opposition of humanity and nature into a unified vision.[8]

The reconciliation of oppositions also occurs with the image of a flower in Noguchi's *noh* play "The Morning-Glory," as is the consummation of love between the estranged lovers symbolized by the climactic dance of the Rainbow Skirt and Feather Jacket in his other *noh* play, "The Everlasting Sorrow."[9] In "The Morning-Glory," the Priest at the end of the play speaks to the Lady, the personification of a flower:

> "Poor child, there is no life where is no death:
> Death is nothing but the turn or change of note.
> The shortest life is the sweetest, as is the shortest song:
> How to die well means how to live well.
> Life is no quest of Longevity and days:
> Where are the flowers a hundred years old?
> O, live in death and Nirvana, live in dissolution and rest,
> Make a life out of death and darkness;
> Lady or flower, be content, be finished as a song that is sung!"

> (*Spirit of Japanese Poetry* 70)

3

Yeats's adaptation from the *noh* play is not only in structure and technique but also in style. His borrowing of the conventions and devices from *noh* is apparent in his stage directions included in the text as well in the notes written separately, but the stylistic influences of the Japanese poetics on Yeats's writing are subtle. To define Japanese characteristics in his style would be to find fine distinctions between his earlier style and that of his later period as a result of his familiarity with the *noh* drama.

His *Autobiography* (1938) makes it clear that his early poetry was aesthetic. His poetical style was the product of the emotionalism associated with the *fin de siècle*, as well as of late nineteenth-century impressionism. Because he was not altogether content with the conventional refinement and genteelness of English aestheticism, he was eager to vitalize his style as he was introduced to the *noh* play. The language of *noh* is consistently devoid of embellishment and tautology; the aim of a great *noh* dramatist like Zeami is to seek the profound beauty in expression influenced neither by the wishful thinking of the writer nor by the fashion of the day. Yeats recognized this mode of expression when he studied certain *noh* dances with Japanese players.[10] What he noticed was "their ideal of beauty, unlike that of Greece and like that of pictures from Japan and China" (*Classic Noh Theatre* 158).

In writing *At the Hawk's Well*, Yeats attempted to adapt a style of tension and intensity that is characteristic of the *noh* structure and of the *noh* dance in particular. The dramatic power of this play lies in the opening lines sung by the musicians as they unfold a piece of cloth, which symbolizes the well. The verse is direct and taut, the image clear, and the song rhythmic:

> I call to the eye of the mind
> A well long choked up and dry
> And boughs long stripped by the wind,
> And I call to the mind's eye
> Pallor of an ivory face,
> A man climbing up to a place
> The salt sea wind has swept bare.

(*Plays of Yeats* 399)

The vividness and intensity of imagery can also be seen in Yeats's later poetry, such as "Byzantium":

> Where blood-begotten spirits come
> And all complexities of fury leave,

Passion and violence thus coalesce into the unified and intensified image of a dance:

> Dying into a dance,
> An agony of trance,
> An agony of flame that cannot singe a sleeve.

(*Poems of Yeats* 248)

The symbolic use of a dance also occurs in Noguchi's English poem "Hagoromo," a summary translation of the well-known *noh Hagoromo*.[11] Pound made a poetic translation of the play into English, based on Fenollosa's notes, and incorporated it into his *Cantos*.[12] Noguchi, on the other hand, renders the scene of the dance in a prose poem:

> The fisherman blushed hugely from shame, and restored the robe to the angel. The angel in her waving robe, with every secret and charm of clouds and sky, with Spring and beauty, began to dance: the fisherman cried in raptuous delight, "Behold! Behold!" The angel sung: "And

then in the Heavens of melody and peace, a place of glory and Love was built by magic hands: it bears the name of Moon. . . . I now stray from the golden sphere, and show the heavenly dance to Mankind. . . ."

The air overflowed with dreams: the Heavens and earth joined their arms and hearts. O angel, dance on through the purple hours: Oh, dance on, fair maiden, while the heavenly flowers crown thy tresses in odorous breeze: O beauteous angel, dance on in Life and Love! (*Summer Cloud* 1–4)

The metaphor of dance used by Yeats and Noguchi, an increased dramatic intensity in poems of dialogue, is adapted from the *noh* play.

The element of style most pervasive in the language of *noh* is called in Japanese *yugen*, an aesthetic principle originated in Zen metaphysics. *Yugen*, as noted earlier, designates the mysterious and dark, what underlies the surface. The mode of expression is subtle as opposed to obvious, suggestive rather than declarative. The fisherman in Noguchi's "Hagoromo," watching the complete performance of a dance as promised by the angel, is left with the feeling of *yugen*:

The angel abruptly stopped, and looked on the fisherman, and with a pretty little bow (like that of a drowsy rose) said: "'Tis the time I have to return home; farewell, dear man!" She soon caught the zephyr from Paradise: her feather robe winged Heavenward. What a strangely splendid sight! And she vanished beyond the clouds and mortal reach. The fisherman stupidly looked round over the empty sea. The singing wind passed amid the pines of the dreamy shore. (*Summer Cloud* 4–5)

Such a scene conveys a feeling of satisfaction and release as does the catharsis of a Greek play, but *yugen* differs from catharsis because it has little to do with the emotional stress caused by tragedy. *Yugen* functions in art as a means by which one can comprehend the course of nature; it is an enlightenment that transcends time and place, and even the consciousness of self. The style of *yugen* can express either happiness or sorrow. Cherry blossoms, however beautiful they may be, must fade away; love between man and woman is inevitably followed by sorrow.

This mystery and elusion, which surrounds the order of the universe, had a strong appeal to Yeats. The hawk at the climax of Yeats's *noh* play performs an enigmatic dance, luring away the young man and inducing the old man to sleep. The dance is a symbol of the mysterious and elusive forces of the universe that thwart desire for immortality and knowledge. When Cuchulain hears the cry of the hawk for the first time, he utters, "It sounded like the sudden cry of a hawk, / but there's no wing in sight." During the dance, while he is mesmerized by the hawk's demeanor, the chorus sings in his behalf, "O god, protect me / From a horrible deathless body / Sliding through the veins of a sudden" (*Plays of Yeats* 406–10). As Noguchi's dancer in "Hagoromo" "vanished beyond the clouds and mortal reach," Yeats's bird "seemed to vanish away" whenever Cuchulain approached her.

Noguchi attributes the principle of *yugen* to the ghostliness of Buddhism. "The *No*," he says, "is the creation of the age when, by virtue of sutra or the Buddha's holy name, any straying ghosts or spirits in Hades were enabled to enter Nirvana" (*Spirit of Japanese Poetry* 66). As an illustration he cites a Japanese *noh* play called *Yama Uba*, or *Mountain Elf*, in which the author, a learned Buddhist priest, portrays how mortals are confused in "a maze of transmigration."[13] Noguchi describes the ending of the play, "after making her prayer to the Elf, the dancer disappears over mountains and mountains, as her life's cloud of perplexity is now cleared away, and the dusts of transmigration are well swept," and adds, "This little play would certainly make a splendid subject for a modern interpretation" (*Spirit of Japanese Poetry* 66–67).

Although Yeats's *noh* play at times carries religious overtones as does the Japanese *noh*, his mode of perception seldom reflects the religious belief. In *Calvary*, where the two principal dialogues of Christ with Lazarus and of Christ with Judas are presented, the focus of the play is on the story of human beings. In the notes, Yeats writes, "I have used my bird-symbolism in these songs to increase the objective loneliness of Christ by contrasting it with a loneliness, opposite in kind, that unlike His can be, whether joyous or sorrowful, sufficient to itself." Yeats's emphasis is not on Christ but on "the images of those He cannot save"; the birds thus signify "Lazarus and Judas and the Roman soldiers for whom He has died in vain." Departing from the Scripture, Yeats deliberately uses birds as symbols of subjective life: "Certain birds, especially as I see things, such lonely birds as the heron, hawk, eagle, and swan, are the natural symbols of subjectivity, especially when floating upon the wind alone or alighting upon some pool or river, while the beasts that run upon the ground, especially those that run in packs, are the natural symbols of objective man" (*Plays of Yeats* 789–90).

For Yeats, then, *yugen* is a purely aesthetic principle with which the natural symbols of subjectivity are presented. "Subjective men," Yeats further comments, "are the more lonely the more they are true to type, seeking always that which is unique or personal" (789). This manner of perception about the lonely flight of the bird exactly corresponds to the style of expression reminiscent of *noh*, a kind of veiled, melancholic beauty full of mystery and depth. In Yeats's *The Dreaming of the Bones*, which in its structure closely resembles the *noh* play *Nishikigi*, a young man describes the dance performed by the lovers Diarmuid and Derorgilla at the climax:

> So strangely and so sweetly. All the ruin,
> All, all their handiwork is blown away
> As though the mountain air had blown it away
> Because their eyes have met. They cannot hear,
> Being folded up and hidden in their dance.
> They have drifted in the dance from rock to rock.
> They have raised their hands as though to snatch the sleep
> That lingers always in the abyss of the sky
> Though they can never reach it. A cloud floats up
> And covers all the mountain-head in a moment;
> And now it lifts and they are swept away.
>
> (*Plays of Yeats* 774–75)

The consummation of love celebrated in this play epitomizes the poetics of *yugen*, for "the aim of the Noh play," Noguchi asserts in *The Egoist*, "is to express a desire of yearning, not for beauty, but for the beauty we dream" ("Everlasting Sorrow" 99). The success of the *noh* play, therefore, depends not so much on the truth of history or humanity as on the attainment of what Edgar Allan Poe called "a portion of that Loveliness whose very elements, perhaps, appertain to eternity alone" (*Selected Writings* 470).

4

This concept of beauty was instrumental in drawing Yeats's interest to Japanese poetics. Historically, the influences of *noh* on Yeats's style was inevitable. Yeats was deeply impressed with the *noh* drama because he found himself in the age of realism. "I am bored and wretched, a limitation I greatly regret," he complained, when the artist seemed to him "no longer a human being but an invention of science" (*Classic Noh Theatre* 152). Yeats did not merely attempt to imitate *noh* plays but succeeded in adapting the form to his own purposes. His aim was to restore the Irish legends as Zeami yearned for the lost world of the Heian period when Japanese literature achieved its elegance.

Yeats, however, was not the earliest writer in modern times who came in close contact with Japanese literature. Lafcadio Hearn, disheartened by the onslaught of modern civilization, was inspired by the mysticism of Japanese Buddhism. Ernest Fenollosa, originally interested in Japanese visual arts, was the first to interpret the *noh* play for the West. And Ezra Pound, strongly influenced by Japanese poetry and by haiku in particular, launched the movement of imagism. These predecessors of Yeats, whose writings had undoubtedly a significant role in Yeats's introduction to Japanese art and literature, were, as was Yeats himself, all looking in from outside. But Yone Noguchi, whose prolific writings in English as well as in Japanese have made a lasting contribution to the East-West literary confluence in modern times, was the only writer deeply ingrained in both traditions.

Whether or not Yeats learned more from Noguchi than from any other contemporary is debatable. What is well understood, however, is that Noguchi throughout his career as a poet and a critic had a stronger affinity for Yeats than for any other poet in the West. In "A Japanese Note on Yeats," published in 1922 as a testimony to Yeats's poetry, Noguchi wrote, "When I admire the Irish literature as I do, it is in its independent aloofness from the others, sad but pleasing like an elegy heard across the seas of the infinite. . . . In its telling of visions and numberless dreams, I see the passionate flame burning to Eternity and deathlessness" (*Through the Torii* 114–15). This bringing of the rich oppositions of joy and sorrow, life and death, into a unified and eternal vision Noguchi saw in Yeats was also what Yeats discovered in the Japanese *noh* play.

CHAPTER 5

EZRA POUND, IMAGISM, AND JAPANESE POETICS

1

It is commonplace to say that imagism played a crucial role in poetic modernism and that Ezra Pound, more than anyone else, put this poetics to practice in the 1910s. Yet imagism still remains a somewhat cloudy topic. Many discussions content themselves with restatements of Pound's celebrated essay on vorticism, published in September 1914 ("Vorticism" 461–71). Even Hugh Kenner, the most eminent critic of Pound, says, "The history of the Imagist Movement is a red herring." He admonishes one "to keep one's eyes on Pound's texts, and avoid generalities about Imagism" (Kenner 58).

In his "Vorticism" essay, Pound acknowledged for the first time in his career his indebtedness to the spirit of Japanese poetry in general and the technique of *hokku*, an older term of haiku, in particular. Among the Poundians, and there have been many in the East and in the West who have tried to reconstruct the historical set of circumstances in which Pound moved, Earl Miner gives the best account of the profound influences that Japanese poetry had on Pound's early writing. It is Miner who offers the best annotated evidence that the sources for Pound's interest in Japanese poetics were partly provided by Pound's fellow Imagists, such as T. E. Hulme, F. S. Flint, and Richard Aldington.[1]

It is Miner as well who most frequently comments on the role Yone Noguchi played in the introduction and interpretation of Japanese poetry to the English audience during the early decades of the twentieth century.[2] As noted earlier, Noguchi was indeed a well-known bilingual Japanese and American poet, who by 1915 had published not only books of criticism widely read in England and America (*The Spirit of Japanese Poetry* and *The Spirit of Japanese Art*), but also several collections of his own English poems. By this date, moreover, his poems had been praised by Willa Cather, Joaquin Miller, and Gelett Burgess in America, by Bliss Carman in Canada, and by George Meredith, William Rossetti, Thomas Hardy, and others in England. What is surprising, therefore, is Miner's dismissive treatment of Noguchi's English writings as having had little to do with the Imagist movement and with Pound in particular.

2

As Pound explained in his essay, the image is not a static, rational idea: "It is a radiant node or cluster; it is what I can, and must perforce, call a VORTEX, from which, and through which, and into which ideas are constantly rushing. In decency one can only call it a VORTEX. And from this necessity came the name 'vorticism'" ("Vorticism" 469–70). A year later, Pound defined the form of an image by stating that the image "may be a sketch, a vignette, a criticism, an epigram or anything else you like. It may be impressionism, it may even be very good prose" ("As for Imagisme" 349). An image, he argued, does not constitute simply a picture of something. As a vortex, the image must be "endowed with energy" ("As for Imagisme" 349). Imagism, in turn, is likened to the painter's use of pigment. "The painter," Pound wrote, "should use his colour because he sees it or feels it. I don't much care whether he is representative or non-representative. . . . It is the same in writing poems, the author must use his *image* . . . *not* because he thinks he can use it to back up some creed or some system of ethics or economics" ("Vorticism" 464).

To demonstrate his poetic theory, Pound thought of an image not as a decorative emblem or symbol, but as a seed capable of germinating and developing into another organism. As an illustration he presented what he called "a *hokku*-like sentence" he had written:

> The apparition of these faces in the crowd:
> Petals, on a wet, black bough.

"In a poem of this sort," he explained, "one is trying to record the precise instant when a thing outward and objective transforms itself, or darts into a thing inward and subjective" ("Vorticism" 467). The image of the faces in the crowd is based in immediate experience at a metro station in Paris; it was "a thing outward and objective." Not only did Pound actually see the "thing," but it generated such a sensation that he could not shake it out of his mind. This image, he emphasizes, "transforms itself, or darts into a thing inward and subjective," that is, the image of the "Petals, on a wet, black bough." Imagism is further contrasted to symbolism: "The symbolist's *symbols* have a fixed value, like numbers in arithmetic, like 1, 2, and 7. The imagiste's images have a variable significance, like the signs a, b, and x in algebra" ("Vorticism" 463).

Although Pound's definition is clear enough, the sources for his ideas are hard to determine. Most discussions about the genesis of the Imagist movement are speculative at best. Pound's insistence that an image in poetry must be active rather than passive suggests that a poem is not a description of something, but, as Aristotle had said of tragedy, an action. Pound approaches Aristotelianism in his insistence that the image of the faces in the crowd in his metro poem was not simply a description of his sensation at the station, but an active entity capable of dynamic development. According to his experience, this particular image instantly transformed itself into another image, that of the petals on a wet, black bough. To Pound, the success of this poem resulted from his instantaneous perception of the relatedness between the two entirely different objects.

But Pound's note on the genesis of "In a Station of the Metro" in the "Vorticism" essay makes it clear that there was nothing instantaneous about the composition of this poem. It was in 1911 that Pound, having seen those "beautiful faces" at La Concorde, wrote a thirty-line poem, "and destroyed it because it was what we call work 'of second intensity'" ("Vorticism" 467). Six months later he reduced the longer text to a poem half the length, and still a year later he wrote the final two-line poem. Pound's insistence on the instantaneous perception of the metro images drove him to repeated attempts at recreating the instantaneous images he had perceived a year-and-a-half earlier. Traditionally, the principle of instantaneity and spontaneity is as fundamental for the composition of *hokku* as the same principle is when applied to Zen-inspired painting and calligraphy. In any event his discovery of *hokku* in 1913 to 1914 was, as he says, "useful in getting out of the impasse in which I had been left by my metro emotion" ("Vorticism" 467). To Pound, the most important thing he learned about *hokku* was "this particular sort of consciousness," which he was unable to identify with any version of impressionist art.[3]

Another equally important tenet of imagism calls for directness in expression. The immediate model for this principle was nineteenth-century French prose. Pound did not mention specific English poets but seemed adamantly opposed to Victorian poetry, which he characterized as wordy and rhetorical. Instead he urged his fellow poets "to bring poetry up to the level of prose." "Flaubert and De Maupassant," he believed, "lifted prose to the rank of a finer art, and one has no patience with contemporary poets who escape from all the difficulties of the infinitely difficult art of good prose by pouring themselves into loose verses" ("Vorticism" 462).

The disagreement between Pound and Yeats over whether poetic images should be suggestive or active, discussed in the previous chapter, involves what Noguchi, a poet and critic well acquainted with both poets, felt compelled to write in "What Is a Hokku Poem?" published in London in 1913.[4] In that essay, Noguchi first defined *hokku* as an expression of Japanese poets' "understanding of Nature," or, better put, as a song or chant of "their longing or wonder or adoration toward Mother Nature" that is "never mystified by any cloud or mist like Truth or Beauty of Keats' understanding." Noguchi differentiated between the "suggestive" and subjective coloration of English poetry and the Japanese *hokku*, "distinctly clear-cut like a diamond or star." He argued, "I say that the star itself has almost no share in the creation of a condition even when your dream or vision is gained through its beauty. . . . I value the 'hokku' poem, at least some of them, because of its own truth and humanity simple and plain." Noguchi then analyzed the aim of *hokku*: the *hokku* poet expresses the spirit of nature, rather than the will of man or woman. Noguchi would agree that *hokku* is "suggestive" only if the word *suggestive* means that "truth and humanity are suggestive." He added, "But I can say myself as a poet . . . that your poem would certainly end in artificiality if you start out to be suggestive from the beginning" ("What Is a Hokku Poem?" 355).

Finally, Noguchi based his definition and analysis of aim in Zen philosophy, understood as discipline of the mind: one should not allow one's individuality to control action. Indeed, Zen does not recognize human reality, the existence of good and evil, because this reality is the creation of human will rather than the spirit of nature. Noguchi thus observed that "there is no word in so common use by Western critics as suggestive, which makes more mischief than enlightenment." Although Western critics "mean it quite simply . . . to be a new force or salvation, . . . I say that no critic is necessary for this world of poetry" ("What Is a Hokku Poem?" 355).

By 1918, Pound's vorticist theory had extended to his discussion of Chinese characters. As the correspondence between Pound and Mary Fenollosa, widow of Ernest Fenollosa, indicates, Pound began to receive Fenollosa's manuscripts as early as 1913.[5] Fenollosa's essay "The Chinese Written Character as a Medium for Poetry," posthumously published by Pound in *The Little Review* in 1918, attempted to show that Chinese characters, which Pound called ideograms, derive from visual rather than aural experiences. A Chinese character, Fenollosa noted, signifies an observable action instead of an abstract notion. Unlike a Western word, a phonetic sign, the Chinese character denotes a concrete, natural phenomenon. It, Fenollosa wrote, "is based upon a vivid shorthand picture of the operations of nature. In the algebraic figure and in the spoken word there is no natural connection between thing and sign: all depends upon sheer convention. But the Chinese method follows natural suggestion" (*Chinese Character* 8).

Pound's attempt to verify Fenollosa's theory involved not only his contemporaries, poets and critics living in London in the 1910s, but his own effort to search for ideas in other sources. One of these sources was the Japanese *noh* play, in which Pound became interested through Fenollosa's notes. It is generally understood that Pound's interest in Japanese poetry, especially *hokku*, grew partly through his acquaintance with Fenollosa's writings. None of Fenollosa's writings, however, directly concerns Japanese poetry, let alone *hokku*. Having lived many years in Japan as an art critic, Fenollosa became well versed in Japanese art and literature, but his actual knowledge of the Japanese language was not profound.[6] It is, therefore, inconceivable that Pound became well acquainted with *hokku* through Fenollosa. It is also unlikely that English contemporaries such as T. E. Hulme and F. S. Flint, who are said to have introduced *hokku* to Pound, served his purpose. Pound would not have been able to learn from them the subtle elements of Japanese poetry because they had no firsthand knowledge of the Japanese language.[7]

3

Pound's most likely source of information was Noguchi, as noted earlier. He first corresponded with Pound and then met Pound, along with Yeats, when he gave a series of lectures on Japanese poetry in England in early 1914. The relationship between Pound and Noguchi began in 1911, when Noguchi sent his fifth collection of English poems, *The Pilgrimage* (1908 and 1909) in two volumes, to Pound with a note: "As I am not yet acquainted with your work, I wish you [would] send your books or books which you like to have me read. This little note may sound quite businesslike, but I can promise you that I can do better in my next letter to you." Noguchi also wrote as a postscript, "I am anxious to read not only your poetical work but also your criticism" (Kodama 4). Pound acknowledged receipt of the books and note and thanked him in a letter postmarked September 2, 1911. Pound further wrote, in part, "You are giving us the spirit of Japan, is it not? very much as I am trying to deliver from obscurity certain forgotten odours of Provence & Tuscany. . . . Of your country I know almost nothing—surely if the east & the west are ever to understand each other that understanding must come slowly & come first through the arts. . . . But I might be more to the point if we who are artists should discuss the matters of technique & motive between ourselves. Also if you should write about these matters I would discuss your letters with Mr. Yeats and likewise my answers" (*Collected English Letters* 210–11).

Although Noguchi did not write again to Pound, Noguchi published his essay "What Is a Hokku Poem?" in London in January 1913, as noted earlier. In the meantime three books of criticism by Noguchi appeared during this period: *The Spirit of Japanese Poetry* (1914), *Through the Torii* (1914), and *The Spirit of Japanese Art* (1915). Noguchi was also invited to contribute "The Everlasting Sorrow: A Japanese Noh Play" in 1917 and an article, "The Japanese Noh Play," in 1918 to *The Egoist*.[8] Pound's encouragement was perhaps responsible for the publication of some of Noguchi's own haiku in *The Egoist* and in *Poetry*.

Because his essays and lectures during this period also dealt with Japanese art, Yeats, who was interested in Japanese painting and the *noh* play, became interested in Noguchi's work as well.[9] As Pound's and Yeats's letters to Noguchi indicate, Pound and Yeats not only were close associates themselves, but also were both well acquainted with Noguchi. Despite the active dialogues that occurred between Pound and Noguchi, critics have not seriously considered their relationship. The only critic who has mentioned Noguchi in discussing the Imagist movement regarded Noguchi not as a poet and critic from whose ideas Pound might have benefited, but as one of the poets whom Pound himself influenced (Goodwin 32). Such a preposterous connection is undermined by the simple fact that most of Noguchi's English poems, as Pound noted in his letter to Noguchi, had been published in America and England long before the early 1910s, when Pound and his fellow poets began to discuss imagism among themselves. It is more accurate historically to say that Noguchi influenced Pound rather than the other way around.

Pound had apparently known little about Japanese poetry before he attended the April 1909 meeting of the Poets' Club. This group, headed by T. E. Hulme, was succeeded by another group called *Les Imagistes* or *Des Imagistes*, which Pound led from 1912 to 1914.[10] Although Pound in fact joined the Poets' Club, its sessions did not prove of much inspiration to him. Richard Aldington, who joined in 1911, was more interested in the color prints by Utamaro, Hokusai, and others found in the British Museum than in Japanese poetry.[11] The fact that Pound was more seriously interested in Japanese poetry than was Aldington is indicated by a parody of Pound's metro poem that Aldington published in the January 1915 issue of *The Egoist*.[12] Allen Upward, another member of *Les Imagistes* whom Pound had met in 1911, had some importance for Pound because Upward used the term *whirl-swirl* in his book *The New Word* (1908). Upward, a self-styled intellectual and a poet, had "a powerful and original mind clearly and trenchantly concerned with matters that bear directly on what Pound meant by 'vortex.'"[13] But Upward, who was well read in Confucius and perhaps familiar with Chinese poetry, did not have sufficient knowledge of Japanese poetry, let alone of *hokku*, to influence Pound (Harmer 38).

The degree of Pound's initial interest in *hokku*, therefore, was not entirely clear, for he was much occupied with Provençal poetry and criticism, as his letter to Noguchi indicates. It is quite possible that Pound learned about *hokku* from T. E. Hulme and F. S. Flint, who were experimenting with *hokku* and *tanka*, the thirty-one-syllable Japanese poetic form (Miner, "Pound" 572). The difficulty with this assumption, however, is that Hulme and Flint studied *hokku* through French translators and critics who used the terms *haiku* and *haikai*, more modern words, rather than *hokku*. Most strikingly, neither Pound nor Noguchi referred to the Japanese poem as *haiku* or *haikai*; both consistently called it *hokku* in their writings.

However coincidental this might have been, there are two more pieces of evidence suggesting that Pound might have learned about *hokku* in Noguchi's work. First, as already observed, the essay "What Is a Hokku Poem?"—in which Noguchi declared that poetic images must be active instead of suggestive, direct instead of symbolic, and that the aim of a *hokku* is to understand the spirit of nature rather than to express the will of an individual—was published in *Rhythm* (London) in January 1913, almost two years before Pound's essay "Vorticism." Even Pound's essay "A Few Don'ts," the earliest manifesto on imagism, appeared in the March 1913 issue of *Poetry* (Chicago) two months after Noguchi's essay. Second, Noguchi's book of criticism, *The Spirit of Japanese Poetry*, was published in London by John Murray in March 1914, half a year before Pound's "Vorticism" essay.[14]

Moreover, the key chapter of Noguchi's book, titled "The Japanese Hokku Poetry," was a lecture delivered in the Hall of Magdalen College, Oxford, on January 28, 1914, at the invitation of Robert Bridges, the poet laureate, and T. H. Warren, president of the college and professor of poetry at the university. The first chapter, "Japanese Poetry," was also based on a lecture Noguchi gave at the Japan Society of London on January 14, 1914. The rest of the book had been presented as other lectures to such audiences as the Royal Asiatic Society and the Quest Society in England before April 1914, when Noguchi left London for Tokyo by way of Paris, Berlin, and Moscow. It is altogether possible that Pound heard Noguchi lecture at the Quest Society since Pound, Wyndham Lewis, and T. E. Hulme all lectured there in 1914.[15] During this stay in England, *Through the Torii*, another collection of essays that included a variety of commentary on William Rossetti, James Whistler, W. B. Yeats, and Oscar Wilde, and his autobiography, *The Story of Yone Noguchi Told by Himself*, also appeared in print.

It is most intriguing that Pound's "Vorticism" essay quoted a famous *hokku* by Moritake just before discussing the often-quoted metro poem:

> The fallen blossom flies back to its branch:
> A butterfly.

> ("Vorticism" 467)

This *hokku* in Japanese has three lines:

> Rak-ka eda ni
> Kaeru to mireba
> Kocho-o kana

Noguchi translated this poem in three lines:

> I thought I saw the fallen leaves
> Returning to their branches:
> Alas, butterflies were they.

> (*Spirit of Japanese Poetry* 50)

Pound must have reconstructed the *hokku* in two lines simply because he had in mind "a form of super-position" in which his metro poem was to be composed. The similarities between Pound's and Noguchi's versions of the poem in question do not seem coincidental, because the superpository division is indicated by a colon in both constructions. Both translations have identical key words: "fallen," "branch," and "butterfly." The only difference in diction is between Pound's "blossom" (*ka* in Japanese) and Noguchi's "leaves." In syntax, however, these translations are different: Noguchi's version is subjective from the start and ends objectively; the reverse is true in Pound's rendering. Syntactically, Noguchi's version is closer to the Japanese original than Pound's. A literal translation of Moritake's first two lines, "Rak-ka eda ni / Kaeru to mireba," would read, "The fallen blossom appears to come back to its branch."

What appealed to Pound was the terseness and intensity of imagery in a *hokku*. Irked by the decorative and superfluous style of much Victorian poetry, he urged his fellow poets to eliminate words that do not contribute to the central meaning of the poem. "All poetic language," Pound insisted, "is the language of exploration. Since the beginning of bad writing, writers have used images as ornaments" ("Vorticism" 466). By saying, "Great literature is simply language charged with meaning to the utmost possible degree," he meant to elaborate the Imagist principle that using fewer words maximizes and intensifies meaning.[16] In "What Is a Hokku Poem?" Noguchi wrote, "I always thought that the most beautiful flowers grow close to the ground, and they need no hundred petals for expressing their own beauty; how can you call it real poetry if you cannot tell it by a few words?" (355).

Pound, furthermore, applied the principle of terseness and intensity to the construction of a single image in his poetry. "The 'one image poem,'" Pound noted, "is a form of super-position, that is to say it is one idea set on top of another. I found it useful in getting out of the impasse in which I had been left by my metro emotion" ("Vorticism" 467). Noguchi pointed out the same technique: "*Hokku* means literally a single utterance or the utterance of a single verse; that utterance should be like a 'moth light playing on reality's dusk,' or 'an art hung, as a web, in the air of perfume,' swinging soft in music of a moment" (*Spirit of Japanese Poetry* 39). To illustrate his point, Noguchi quoted a *hokku* by Buson:

> The night of the Spring,—
> Oh, between the eve
> And the dawn.

This *hokku* was placed against the opening passage of *Makura no Soshi* (*Pillow Sketches*) by Sei Shonagon (966?–1025?), a celebrated prose writer in medieval Japan: "I love to watch the dawn grow gradually white and whiter, till a faint rosy tinge crowns the mountain's crest, while slender streaks of purple cloud extend themselves above." Noguchi considered Buson's image far more vivid and intensive than Sei Shonagon's, remarking, "Buson is pleased to introduce the night of the Spring which should be beautiful without questioning, since it lies between those two beautiful things, the eve and the dawn" (*Spirit of Japanese Poetry* 48–49).

4

Not only was Noguchi an interpreter of *hokku* poems for the English reader, but he tried his hand at writing *hokku* poems in English. He later collected them in the volume *Japanese Hokkus* (1920), which he dedicated to Yeats.[17] One of Noguchi's earliest *hokku* is reminiscent of Buson's, quoted above:

> Tell me the street to Heaven.
> This? Or that? Oh, which?
> What webs of streets!
>
> ("What Is a Hokku Poem?" 358)

He wrote this *hokku* in England, he says, "when I most abruptly awoke in 1902 to the noise of Charing Cross. . . . And it was by Westminster Bridge where I heard the evening chime that I wrote again in 'hokku' which appears, when translated, as follows" ("What Is a Hokku Poem?" 358):

> Is it, Oh, list:
> The great voice of Judgment Day?
> So runs Thames and my Life.[18]

Noguchi wrote many *hokku*-like poems like these in imitation of the Japanese *hokku*, as did Pound. The superpository technique, which Pound said he had discovered in Japanese *hokku*, resembles that of Noguchi. For instance, Pound's "Alba," typical of his many *hokku*-like poems, reads,

As cool as the pale wet leaves
of lily-of-the-valley
She lay beside me in the dawn.

(*Personae* 109)

Most of Noguchi's *hokku*, as the two poems quoted above show, do
have a form of superposition. Like Pound's, Noguchi's *hokku* constitutes one image poem which has two separate ideas set on top of
one another. In the first poem by Noguchi, an idea of "the street to
Heaven" is set on top of an idea of "webs," despite a close similarity
between the two images. In the second, an idea of the flow of the
Thames is set on top of an idea of the course of "my Life."

But there are some differences between Noguchi's and Pound's
hokku. Noguchi does not as closely adhere to the well-established Japanese syllabic measure of five or seven as does Pound. Noguchi's two
hokku above have 7-5-4 and 4-7-6 measures; Pound's "Alba," "Fan-
Piece, for Her Imperial Lord," and "Ts'ai Chi'h" have those of 7-7-8,
7-5-7, and 8-7-7, respectively. If the first line of Pound's metro poem
had been reconstructed as two lines, the poem would have had a measure of 5-7-7 ("The apparition / Of these faces in the crowd / Petals
on a wet, black bough"), much like a Japanese *hokku*. Noguchi, moreover, tends to ignore the long-established poetic tradition in which a
Japanese *hokku* has an explicit reference to a season. Pound, on the
other hand, consciously adheres to this tradition as seen in many of his
hokku-like poems and somewhat longer pieces such as "Heather" and
"Society" (*Personae* 109–11).

What a Japanese *hokku* and Pound's image share besides their brevity and intensity is the poet's ability to escape the confinement of
the poem. The sense of liberation in *hokku* is usually accomplished
through references to time and space. A Japanese *hokku* contains not
only a reference to a season, an indication of time, but an image of
nature, that of space. Pound's *hokku*-like poems, such as "In a Station
of the Metro" and "Alba," indeed have references to time and space.
Pound called the metro emotion, which came from the image of the
faces in the crowd, "a thing outward and objective," and the image
of the petals, on a wet, black bough "a thing inward and subjective."
The image of the petals, nevertheless, is a natural object in contrast to
that of the faces in the crowded station, a human object.

In Pound's mind—in the realm of subjective perception—the
image of the faces, an objective image, transforms into the image of

the petals, a subjective image. This perception also means that the image of the faces, an image of people, transforms into that of the petals, an image of nature. The shifting of objective and subjective images in Pound's poem is depicted in terms of a vortex, in which an image is not only active in itself but also capable of merging into another image that appears in its wake. Because Pound's image has this tendency, it is often as difficult to separate the mental vision from the external as it is to separate mind from matter, the perceiver from the perceived, in Japanese *hokku*.

In *The Spirit of Japanese Poetry*, Noguchi is as critical as Pound of the Western poet's tendency to wordiness. Noguchi's emphasis on the Japanese *hokku* as "the real poetry of action" entails that a *hokku* aim to narrow the distance between humanity and nature, the perceiver and the perceived. The narrower the distance, the better the *hokku* becomes. Based on "Lao Tze's canon of spiritual anarchism" and Zen's principle of controlling the mind, Noguchi declares,

> To attach too closely to the subject matter in literary expression is never a way to complete the real saturation; the real infinite significance will only be accomplished at such a consummate moment when the end and means are least noticeable, and the subject and expression never fluctuate from each other, being in perfect collocation; it is the partial loss of the birthright of each that gains an artistic triumph. . . . I do never mean that the *Hokku* poems are lyrical poetry in the general Western understanding; but the Japanese mind gets the effect before perceiving the fact of their brevity, its sensibility resounding to their single note, as if the calm bosom of river water to the song of a bird. (*Spirit of Japanese Poetry* 34)

To illustrate what he calls "the sense of mystical affinity between the life of Nature and the life of man, between the beauty of flowers and the beauty of love," he quotes his own poem, as discussed in Chapter 3 on Noguchi:

> It's accident to exist as a flower or a poet:
> A mere twist of evolution but from the same force;
> I see no form in them but only beauty in evidence;
> It's the single touch of their imagination to get the embodiment
>   of a poet or
> a flower:
> To be a poet is to be a flower,
> To be the dancer is to make the singer sing. (37)

Pound, on the other hand, views the affinity between humanity and nature differently. What Pound calls "a thing inward and subjective" does not necessarily correspond to a vision of a person; nor is "a thing outward and objective" the same thing as a vision of nature.

This fusion of humanity and nature is called spontaneity in Zen. The best *hokku* poems, because of their linguistic limitations, are inwardly extensive and outwardly infinite. A severe constraint imposed on one aspect of *hokku* must be balanced by a spontaneous, boundless freedom on the other. From a Zen point of view, such a vision is devoid of thought and emotion. Since Zen is the most important philosophical tradition influencing Japanese *hokku*, the *hokku* poet aims at understanding the spirit of nature. Basho, a Zen-inspired poet, recognizes little division between humanity and nature, the subjective and the objective; he is never concerned with the problems of good and evil. Placed against this tradition, Pound's poetics in its philosophical aspect considerably differs from Basho's. Pound cannot be called a Zen poet because he declared, "An 'Image' is that which presents an intellectual and emotional complex in an instant of time" (*Literary Essays* 4). A Zen poet seeks satori, an enlightenment that transcends time and place and even the consciousness of self. This enlightenment is defined as a state absolutely free of any thought or emotion, a state that corresponds to that of nature. For a Zen-inspired poet, nature is a mirror of the enlightened self; one must see and hear things as they really are by making one's consciousness pure and clear. Pound seems to be able to appreciate this state of mind, but obviously he does not necessarily try to seek it in his own work.

In fact, Japanese traditional haiku do not take sexual love, illness, and natural disaster for their subjects. And while Pound's poetry does express good and evil, love and hatred, individual feeling and collective myth, Basho's shuns such sentiments and emotions altogether. Pound and a Zen poet, however, do agree that their poetic vision is spontaneous and capable of attaining enlightenment. Pound maintained, "It is the presentation of such a 'complex' instantaneously which gives that sense of sudden liberation; that sense of freedom from time and space limits; that sense of sudden growth, which we experience in the presence of the greatest works of art" (*Literary Essays* 4). Pound's observation, however, is very much a Western formulation of an experience familiar to Zen-inspired artists.

This sense of liberation suggests an impersonal conception of poetry, for it focuses attention not on the poet but on the image. T. S. Eliot, whom most observers agree Pound influenced, held the same view (*Selected Essays* 8–10). Japanese poets such as Basho, Buson, and

Issa held the same principle. Their poetry seldom dealt with dreams, fantasies, or concepts of heaven and hell; it was strictly concerned with the portrayal of nature—mountains, trees, flowers, birds, animals, insects, waterfalls, nights, days, seasons. For the Japanese *hokku* poet, nature is a mirror of the enlightened self; the poet must see and hear things as they really are by making his or her consciousness pure, natural, and unemotional. "Japanese poets," Noguchi wrote, "go to Nature to make life more meaningful, sing of flowers and birds to make humanity more intensive" (*Spirit of Japanese Poetry* 37).

As opposed to his later poetry, Pound's early poetry, and his *hokku*-like poems in particular, have little to do with his personal emotion or thought. In such poetry, Pound is not really concerned with thought and emotion. If Pound's *hokku* sounded intellectual or emotional, it did so only to an English reader who was still Arnoldian in his or her taste and unfamiliar with the Imagist movement of the 1910s, not to mention with "the spirit of Japanese poetry" Noguchi tried to introduce to the English audience. Japanese poetry shuns symbols and metaphors because figurative language might lessen the intensity and spontaneity of a newly experienced sensation. Such expressions would not only undermine originality in the poet's sensibility, but resort to intellectualization—as well as what Noguchi, perhaps echoing Matthew Arnold, called "a criticism of life," which traditionally Japanese poetry was not (*Through the Torii* 159).

The *hokku* poet may not only aim at expressing sensation but also at generalizing and hence depersonalizing it. This characteristic can be shown even by one of Basho's lesser-known *hokku*, as noted earlier:

> How cool it is!
> Putting the feet on the wall:
> An afternoon nap.[19]

In "Alba," what Pound expressed was not the personal feeling he had about the woman lying beside him at dawn, but his spontaneous sensation of the coolness of "the pale wet leaves / of lily-of-the-valley." Likewise, the sensation of slowly cooling hot water was Pound's subject in "The Bath Tub," as the title suggests, rather than his feelings about the woman (*Personae* 100). The image of a "fan of white silk, / clear as frost on the grass-blade" is central in "Fan-Piece, for Her Imperial Lord," where a minimal image of the lord's concubine is evoked by a one-word reference to her: "You also are laid aside" (*Personae* 108). Such subtleties could not have been learned from Pound's fellow Imagists like Flint and Aldington. These Imagists remained labored, superficial imitators of Japanese *hokku*. Pound and Noguchi, by contrast, showed themselves far more capable of understanding the spirit of Japanese poetry.

5

As partly suggested in the previous remarks on superposition, the *hokku* also provided a structural model for Pound's version of imagism. Acknowledging that the Japanese had evolved this short form of poetry, Pound seized on the unique form of "super-position" which, he observed, constitutes a *hokku*. To him, the *hokku* often consists of two disparate images in juxtaposition, and yet it appears as a single image. Lacking the copula *is* or the preposition *like*, the image cannot be metaphoric or analogical. As Pound's account of the composition of the metro poem shows, he had no intention of likening the image of the beautiful faces in the crowd to the image of petals on a wet, black bough or of making one image suggestive or representative of the other.[20] If one image is used to suggest another or to represent another, both images would be weakened. But if one image is used to generate or intensify another, and the other image, in turn, intensifies the first one, then the whole poem as one image would be intensified.

The key to the superpository structure of Pound's image is a coalescence of two unlike images. Such an image must be generated "in an instant of time," as Pound cautions in his essay "A Few Don'ts" (*Literary Essays* 4). Creating such an image needs no preparations, no explanations, no qualifications; Pound calls "the 'natural course of events' the exalted moment, the vision unsought or at least the vision gained without machination" (*Spirit of Romance* 97). In *The Spirit of Japanese Poetry* and *The Spirit of Romance*, Noguchi and Pound, respectively, emphasized this revelatory moment when high poetry must be written. But such a parallel in their poetics does not necessitate that one's ideas came from the other's. Pound's observations might have been made independently.

It is quite possible that Pound became acquainted through other sources with many of the superpository *hokku* that Noguchi cited as examples in *The Spirit of Japanese Poetry*. In addition to Moritake's "I Thought I Saw the Fallen Leaves" and Basho's "The Old Pond," Noguchi translated the following: Buson's "Oh, How Cool—" (47) and "Prince Young, Gallant" (36), Basho's "Lying Ill on Journey" (38), and Hokushi's "It Has Burned Down" (27). It may be significant, however, that in another collection of critical essays, Noguchi cited several of his own numerous *hokku* in English along with those by old masters. Many of Noguchi's English *hokku*, moreover, had been published in *The Pilgrimage* (1908, 1909). Pound might have acquainted himself with Noguchi's published *hokku* before he experimented with his version.

As Pound accounted for the circumstances of his metro poem in Paris in 1912, Noguchi also narrated the experience he had had in London in 1903:

> I myself was a *hokku* student since I was fifteen or sixteen years old; during many years of my Western life, now amid the California forest, then by the skyscrapers of New York, again in the London 'bus, I often tried to translate the *hokku* of our old masters but I gave up my hope when I had written the following in English:

> > My Love's lengthened hair
> > Swings o'er me from Heaven's gate:
> > Lo, Evening's shadow!

> It was in London, to say more particularly, Hyde Park, that I wrote the above *hokku* in English, where I walked slowly, my mind being filled with the thought of the long hair of Rossetti's woman as I perhaps had visited Tate's Gallery that afternoon. . . . I exclaimed then: "What use to try the impossibility in translation, when I have a moment to feel a *hokku* feeling and write about it in English?"[21]

Structurally, Pound's metro poem resembles Noguchi's Hyde Park *hokku*. As in Pound's poem, where the outward image of the faces in the crowd is set on top of the inward image of petals on a wet, black bough, so the actual vision of an evening shadow in Noguchi's poem is juxtaposed to an envisioning of a woman's long hair. In each poem a pair of images, similar in form but different in content, coalesces into another autonomous image, which generates different meaning. The superposition of the paired images transforms into a different image in form and content, what Pound calls "the 'one image' poem" ("Vorticism" 467). This transformation of images retains the sensation of each separate object perceived, but it also conveys a greater sensation by uniting the two experiences.[22] For both poets, such a transformation is optimal, for they believe that images in poetry cannot and should not be divided as external and internal, physical and mental, objective and subjective.[23]

To illustrate the energy latent in this transformation of images, Pound provided an anecdote: "I once saw a small child go to an electric light switch and say, 'Mamma, can I *open* the light?' She was using the age-old language of exploration, the language of art" ("Vorticism" 466). Although he later became interested in Fenollosa's explanation that written Chinese characters denote action, he was first attracted to the poetics of the *hokku*, what he called "the sense of exploration . . . the beauty of this sort of knowing" ("Vorticism" 466–67). Noguchi expounded this poetics in terms of an intensive art by referring to Kikaku's celebrated *hokku*, as discussed earlier:

> Autumn's full moon:
> Lo, the shadows of a pine tree
> Upon the mats!

The beauty of the harvest moon is not only humanized but intensified by the shadow of a tree Kikaku saw on the *tatami* mats. "Really," Noguchi wrote, "it was my first opportunity to observe the full beauty of the light and shadow, more the beauty of the shadow in fact, far more luminous than the light itself, with such a decorativeness, particularly when it stamped the dustless mats as a dragon-shaped ageless pine tree" ("What Is a Hokku Poem?" 357). The situation here, shared by Pound and Noguchi, is one of finding, discovering, and hence inventing the new.

As if to bear out Pound's vorticist thinking in poetry, Noguchi made a modest proposal for English poets. "I think," he wrote, "it is time for them to live more of the passive side of Life and Nature, so as to make the meaning of the whole of them perfect and clear." To the Japanese mind, an intensive art can be created not from action, but from inaction. Noguchi thus argued that the larger part of life "is builded upon the unreality by the strength of which the reality becomes intensified" (*Spirit of Japanese Poetry* 24–25). Noguchi's paradox was echoed in Pound's statement about vorticism. To Pound, an intensive art is not an emphatic art. By an intensive art, Pound meant that "one is concerned with the relative intensity, or relative significance, of different sorts of expression. . . . They are more dynamic. I do not mean they are more emphatic, or that they are yelled louder" ("Vorticism" 468).

Pound illustrated this intensive art with a *hokku*-like sentence in his essay "Affirmations," first published in the *New Age* in 1915:

> The pine-tree in mist upon the far hill looks
> like a fragment of Japanese armour.

The images appear in simile form, but Pound has no intention of intensifying the beauty of either image by comparing it to that of the other. "In either case," he points out, "the beauty, in so far as it is beauty of form, is the result of 'planes in relation.' . . . The tree and the armour are beautiful because their diverse planes overlie in a certain manner." Unlike the sculptor or the painter, the poet, who must use words to intensify his art, Pound says, "may cast on the reader's mind a more vivid image of either the armour or the pine by mentioning them close together . . . for he works not with planes or with colours but with the names of objects and of properties. It is his business so to use, so to arrange, these names as to cast a more definite image than the layman can cast" (*Gaudier-Brzeska* 120–21).

Critics have shown over the years that Pound's idea of vorticism underlies not only his short imagistic poems, but also his longer pieces such as the *Cantos, Cathay*, and his translation of *noh* plays. Noguchi, on the other hand, attempted to intensify an image in a poem longer than the *hokku* by endowing it with action and autonomy. "The Passing of Summer" (1909), for instance, reads,

> An empty cup whence the light of passion is drunk!—
> To-day a sad rumour passes through the trees,
> A chill wind is borne by the stream,
> The waves shiver in pain;
> Where now the cicada's song long and hot?

> (*Pilgrimage* 1: 68)

Such visual images as an empty cup, the chilly wind blowing over the stream, and the shivering waves do not simply denote the passing of summer; they constitute its action. Similarly, experiences or memories of experiences like drinking "the light of passion" and hearing "the cicada's song long and hot" do not merely express the poet's nostalgia or sentiment about the summer; these images, rather than being metonymies, recreate the actions of the summer itself.[24] In Noguchi's poetry, as in the *hokku*, poetry and sensation are spontaneously conjoined and intensified, to leave no room for rationalism or moralism.

6

Numerous parallels between Pound's poetics and Noguchi's do not entail the conclusion that both poets held the same principles throughout their respective careers. Much of Noguchi's art and literary criticism shows great enthusiasm at times for Yeats's mysticism and Whitman's transcendentalism.[25] Noguchi had a taste for certain styles of poetry that Pound obviously did not. But what their writings as a whole suggest is that both writers, as poets and critics, agreed on the ideas of imagism during the period between 1908, when *The Pilgrimage*, Noguchi's fifth collection of English poems, appeared in Tokyo and London, and 1914, when Noguchi's *The Spirit of Japanese Poetry* was published in London. For Noguchi, this period came in the middle of his career, as it coincided with Pound's early career and interest in imagism. This agreement on imagism constituted an interpenetrating relationship of Japanese poetics and Western intentions in early modernism. Pound's launching of imagism in London in 1912 and 1913 with the support of T. E. Hulme, F. S. Flint, H. D., Richard Aldington, and others has become a legend of sorts. And much of the Imagist work by various hands began to appear in Chicago in *Poetry* and in London in *Des Imagistes* and *The Freewoman* (later *The Egoist*). But the sources that Noguchi brought to Western attention as early as 1903, when *From the Eastern Sea*, the third collection of his English poems, was published in London, have become not only obscure but neglected.

In March 1913, Pound and his associates collectively drew up and published the three principles of their "faith." The first was "direct treatment of the 'thing,' whether subjective or objective." Noguchi would wholeheartedly have endorsed the formulation. The second principle called for "using absolutely no word that does not contribute to the presentation," and Noguchi had documented the practice of this tenet in the *hokku* by Japanese masters as well as in his own work. The third principle was "to compose in sequence of the musical phrase, not in sequence of the metronome" ("Vorticism" 462). Because the Japanese language radically differs from a Western language in rhythm, rhyme, stress, or tone, Noguchi would readily have assented to the proposal.

Much of Pound's early work and Noguchi's clearly reflects this accord between the Imagists and Noguchi. It is true that while Pound was fascinated by Japanese poetics, he was also interested in vorticism as applied to visual arts, as his commentary on such artists as Gaudier-Brzeska, Brancusi, and Picasso indicates. Through the Poets' Club, Pound was also closely associated with Hulme, Flint, Aldington, Upward, and others, some of whom were initially attracted to Japanese color prints by such painters as Utamaro and Hokusai exhibited in the British Museum. There is clear evidence that Pound's associates also tried their hand at *hokku* with various degrees of seriousness and success. By the mid-1910s, imagism had indeed become the literary zeitgeist, and any poet living in London would have received some influence from the Japanese sources.

To sum up, then, Noguchi's English poems had been widely circulated in London well before September 1914, when Pound's vorticism essay appeared, and Noguchi's essay on *hokku* in *Rhythm* and his book *The Spirit of Japanese Poetry* were published in January 1913 and March 1914, respectively. The material in the essay and the book was delivered as a series of lectures during his stay in England from December 1913 to April 1914. In these circumstances, it is hardly conceivable that the Imagists did not acquaint themselves with Noguchi's ideas. Even though Pound's modernist theory might partly have derived from other sources, one can scarcely overlook the direct link between Japanese poetics and Pound's imagism through Noguchi.

CHAPTER 6

JACK KEROUAC'S HAIKU
AND BEAT POETICS

Jack Kerouac (1922–69), whose first novel, *On the Road* (1957), captured a huge audience, played a central role in the literary movement
he named the Beat Generation. His second novel, *The Dharma Bums*
(1958), gave an intimate biographical account of himself in search of
the truth in life. In San Francisco he met Gary Snyder (1930–) and
the two Dharma bums explored the thoughts and practices of Buddhism. As Snyder left for Japan to study at a Zen monastery, Kerouac
reached an apogee on a desolate mountaintop in the Sierras.

The uninhibited story of Kerouac and Snyder on the West Coast
also coincided with the birth of the San Francisco Poetry Renaissance.
Kerouac called the event "the whole gang of howling poets" gathered at Gallery Six. In the beginning of *The Dharma Bums*, Kerouac
described the poetry reading:

> Everyone was there. It was a mad night. And I was the one who got
> things jumping by going around collecting dimes and quarters from
> the rather stiff audience standing around in the gallery and coming
> back with three huge gallon jugs of California Burgundy and getting
> them all piffed so that by eleven o'clock when Alvah Goldbook [Allen
> Ginsberg] was reading his, wailing his poem "Wail" [Howl] drunk with
> arms outspread everybody was yelling "Go! Go! Go!" (like a jam ses-
> sion) and old Rheinhold Cacoethes the father of the Frisco poetry scene
> was wiping his tears in gladness. Japhy [Gary Snyder] himself read his
> fine poems about Coyote the God of the North American Plateau Indi-
> ans (I think), at least the God of the Northwest Indians, Kwakiutl and
> what-all. "Fuck you! sang Coyote, and ran away!" read Japhy to the

distinguished audience, making them all howl with joy, it was so pure, fuck being a dirty word that comes out clean. And he had his tender lyrical lines, like the ones about bears eating berries, showing his love of animals, and great mystery lines about oxen on the Mongolian road showing his knowledge of Oriental literature even on to Hsuan Tsung the great Chinese monk who walked from China to Tibet, Lanchow to Kashgar and Mongolia carrying a stick of incense in his hand. (13–14)

Not only did this inaugural meeting of the Beat Generation feature the three well-known writers Kerouac, Snyder, and Ginsberg (1926–97), the subsequent interactions among them revealed their backgrounds and worldviews. Snyder, born in San Francisco, followed Ginsberg's first reading of "Howl" at this gathering with his own lyrical poems, as mentioned above. Later in *The Dharma Bums*, Snyder observed, "East'll meet West anyway. Think what a great world revolution will take place when East meets West finally, and it'll be guys like us that can start the thing. Think of millions of guys all over the world with rucksacks on their backs tramping around the back country and hitchhiking and bringing the word down to everybody." Kerouac responded by referring to a Christian tradition he remembered as he grew up a Catholic in a French American family in Massachusetts: "That's a lot like the early days of the Crusades, Walter the Penniless and Peter the Hermit leading ragged bands of believers to the Holy Land." Snyder, admonishing Kerouac against believing in his Western legacy, said, "Yeah but that was all such European gloom and crap, I want my Dharma Bums to have springtime in their hearts when the blooms are girling and the birds are dropping little fresh turds surprising cats who wanted to eat them a moment ago" (160).

Discussing Buddhism and Zen philosophy, in particular, with Snyder, as well as reading books on Buddhism in the local libraries, Kerouac realized that Buddhism, rather than denying suffering and death, confronted both. For him, Buddhism taught one to transcend the origin of suffering and death: desire and ignorance. Most impressively, Buddhism taught Kerouac that the phenomenal world was like a dream and an illusion and that happiness consisted in achieving that strange vision in the mind—enlightenment. *The Dharma Bums* also informs that while Snyder was continuously fascinated with Zen, Kerouac was inspired by Mahayana Buddhism. To Kerouac, Zen, which teaches spontaneous, realistic action for human beings, compromises with active, worldly existence. Consequently, Zen admonished against existing in a world of temptation and evil. On the contrary, Kerouac was impressed with Mahayana Buddhism, for one's goal of life is to achieve Buddhahood, a celestial state of enlightenment and acceptance of all forms of life.

The genesis of the Beat movement goes back to the meeting of Kerouac and Ginsberg at Columbia University in the early 1940s. Kerouac and Ginsberg, who grew up in New Jersey of Russian Jewish immigrant parents, also shared their literary interests with William Burroughs (1914–97), who hailed from Missouri. During this period, Kerouac, immersed with American transcendentalism, read Emerson, Thoreau, and Whitman. Kerouac was influenced by Emerson's concept of self-reliance as he learned of Whitman's singular, stubborn independence and refusal to subscribe to society's materialistic, commercial demands. At the same time it was Thoreau's writings, such as *Walden, A Week on the Concord and Merrimack Rivers,* and *Variorum Civil Disobedience* that introduced Kerouac to Confucianism and Buddhism.[1]

Learning about Buddhism from Thoreau, Kerouac became seriously interested in studying its philosophy. His study of Buddhism, then, led to writing *The Dharma Bums.* For Kerouac, Mahayana Buddhism served to change the state of defeat in the world that the Beat movement represented to the beatific acceptance of life the Buddhist texts described. For Gary Snyder, Zen Buddhism transformed the Beats to the Zen Lunatics, who refused "to subscribe to the general demand that they consume production and therefore have to work for the privilege of consuming, all that crap they didn't really want anyway such as refrigerators, TV sets, cars. . . . I see a vision of . . . Zen Lunatics who go about writing poems that happen to appear in their heads for no reason and also by being kind and also by strange unexpected acts keep giving visions of eternal freedom to everybody and to all living creatures" (*Dharma Bums* 77–78).

Kerouac responded, as did Snyder, to the Zen principle to establish authority in one's spontaneous and intuitive insights and actions. Kerouac took pains to see things as they existed without commentary, interpretation, and judgment. For Kerouac, and for the Beat Generation, the Zen perspective made art conform to life itself. A Zen-inspired poet must see whatever happens in life—order and disorder, permanence and change. This Zen principle partly accounts for Kerouac's rejection of the idea of revision.[2] With respect to spontaneous prose, Kerouac stated, "And, Not 'selectivity' of expression but following free deviation (association) of mind into limitless blow-on-subject seas of thought . . . write as deeply, fish down as far as you want, satisfy yourself first, then reader cannot fail to receive telepathic shock and meaning—excitement by same laws operating in his own human mind" ("Essentials of Spontaneous Prose" 73).

Upon publication of *On the Road*, Kerouac was writing haiku. Thanks to Regina Weinreich's edition of *Book of Haikus* by Jack Kerouac (2003), we have a well-detailed account of Kerouac's writing of those several hundred haiku. As mentioned in *The Dharma Bums*, Kerouac, while reading a number of books on Buddhism, also consulted the four-volume book on Japanese haiku by R. H. Blyth, especially the first volume, subtitled "Eastern Culture." "Kerouac's pocket notebooks," as Weinreich notes, contained "haiku entries written in New York City, Tangier, Aix-en-Provence, London, New York City again, Berkeley, Mexico, and Orlando. As the notebooks and letters of this period show, Kerouac exhorted himself to write haiku, mindful of the traditional methods" (*Book of Haikus* 106).

While abiding by the principles and techniques of haiku shown by Blyth, Kerouac realized that an English haiku cannot be composed in seventeen syllables as in Japanese. "Western languages," Kerouac noted, "cannot adapt themselves to the fluid syllabic Japanese. I propose that the 'Western Haiku' simply say a lot in three short lines in any Western language. Above all," he emphasized, "a Haiku must be very simple and free of all poetic trickery and make a little picture and yet be as airy and graceful as a Vivaldi Pastorella." He presented, as examples, three haiku by Basho, Buson, and Issa, saying they are "simpler and prettier than any Haiku I could ever write in any language" (Tonkinson 74):

> A day of quiet gladness,—
> Mount Fuji is veiled
> In misty rain.

> (Basho) (1644–1694)

> The nightingale is singing,
> Its small mouth
> Open.

> (Buson) (1715–1783)

> She has put the child to sleep,
> And now washes the clothes:
> The summer moon.

> (Issa) (1763–1827)

In each of the haiku, two images are juxtaposed: the veiled Mount Fuji and the misty rain in Basho's haiku, the singing nightingale and its open mouth in Buson's, and the mother having put her child to sleep and washing the clothes and the summer moon in Issa's. Kerouac said in his *Paris Review* interview, "A sentence that's short and sweet with a sudden jump of thought is a kind of haiku, and there's a lot of freedom and fun in surprising yourself with that, let the mind willy-nilly jump from the branch to the bird" (Weinreich, *Book of Haikus* xxiv–xxv).

As Kerouac's *Book of Haikus* indicates, Kerouac continuously wrote haiku to render the Beats' worldview. "For a new generation of poets," Weinreich has observed, "Kerouac ended up breaking ground at a pioneering stage of an American haiku movement" (*Book of Haikus* xv). Allen Ginsberg celebrated Kerouac's haiku:

> Kerouac has the one sign of being a great poet, which is he's the only one in the United States who knows how to write haikus. The only one who's written any good haikus. And everybody's been writing haikus. There are all these dreary haikus written by people who think for weeks trying to write a haiku, and finally come up with some dull little thing or something. Whereas Kerouac thinks in haikus, every time he writes anything—talks that way and thinks that way. So it's just natural for him. It's something Snyder noticed. Snyder has to labor for years in a Zen monastery to produce one haiku about shitting off a log! And actually does get one or two good ones. Snyder was always astounded by Kerouac's facility. (Lynch 123–24)

There were, however, some poets who were not enthusiastic about Kerouac's haiku. Lawrence Ferlinghetti, who was associated with the Beat writers and the San Francisco Renaissance poets and who, founding his own press, published his friend Allen Ginsberg's work, said that Kerouac "was a better novel writer than a poem writer" (Gifford and Lee 271).

As many of the classic haiku poets in Japan like Basho were influenced by Confucian thought, so was Kerouac. In the first volume, *Haiku: Eastern Culture*, which Kerouac studied in earnest, Blyth explains that, according to Confucius, the universe consists of heaven, earth, and humans. *The Analects,* a collection of Confucian maxims and parables, contains Confucius's thoughts and observations on the relationships among heaven, humans, and God. For Confucius, God is not a living being like a human being: God is a concept that originated from a human being. The individual living in society must formulate this concept by understanding the ways of nature in heaven and on earth. One is conscious of the supremacy of heaven over earth and humans.

Some of Kerouac's haiku express this worldview, for example,

> Reflected upsidedown,
>   in the sunset lake, pines
> Pointing to infinity

(Book of Haikus 101)

This haiku focuses on an image of the universe that makes human existence infinitesimal, in contrast to an infinite space that represents the universe. The image of pines reflected in the lake bears a resemblance to that of "the sacred pine-tree" in Emerson's poem "The Problem":

> Or how the sacred pine-tree adds
> To her old leaves new myriads?

(Selections 418)

Kerouac is impressed, as is Emerson, with the infinity of the universe. Emerson's argument is that divinity that represents the universe is proven by nature, not by the church or human achievements like huge pyramids in Egypt and ancient temples in Greece. Similarly, Kerouac envisions the scope of the universe by looking at the pines reflected upside down in the sunset lake.[3]

Kerouac's haiku "The Backyard I Tried to Draw" has an affinity with Basho's "The Mountains and Garden Also Move" in its expression of the Confucian worldview:

> The backyard I tried to draw
>   —It still looks
> The same

(Book of Haikus 117)

> The mountains and garden also move;
> The summer drawing-room
>   Includes them.

(Blyth, Haiku 38)

The garden in Basho's haiku represents a space shared by human beings and the earth. So does the backyard in Kerouac's haiku. Both images suggest that despite the human creation of the space, they still belong to the earth, a permanent space under heaven. Similarly, Kerouac's haiku "Dusk—The Blizzard" and Emerson's poem "The Snow-Storm" both express the Confucian worldview:

> Dusk—The blizzard
> > hides everything,
> Even the night

> (*Book of Haikus* 38)

> Announced by all the trumpets of the sky,
> Arrives the snow, and, driving o'er the fields,
> Seems nowhere to alight: the whited air
> Hides hills and woods, the river, and the heaven,
> And veils the farm-house at the garden's end.

> (*Selections* 414)

Both poems depict the supremacy of heaven over the earth and human beings.

The following haiku by Kerouac also describe the control the universe has over the earth and humanity:

> Following each other,
> > my cats stop
> When it thunders

> (*Book of Haikus* 27)

> The summer chair
> > rocking by itself
> In the blizzard

> (36)

In these haiku, the phenomena above the earth and human beings have control over them. The first haiku, "Following Each Other," captures the moment when the thunderstorm halts the cats' movement. In the second haiku, "The Summer Chair," the blizzard rather than a human being is rocking the chair. Another haiku on the same subject, "In the sun / the butterfly wings / Like a church window" (62), suggests that human law must follow the law of the universe. So does the haiku "THE LIGHT BULB / SUDDENLY WENT OUT— / STOPPED READ-ING" (64): at night, without light from the sun, humans cannot see.

Confucianism, as Blyth shows, teaches "the sense of something that feeds the life of man, which can be absorbed into our own life and yet have a life of its own, which is organic and glowing" (*Haiku* 71). Some of Kerouac's haiku convey the Confucian thought that life in whatever form it exists is organic and changeable. For example,

> May grass—
> Nothing much
> To do
>
> (118)

illustrates a phenomenon in nature: May grass, with rain and sun, grows naturally and vigorously. In the following haiku,

> Sex—shaking to breed
> as
> Providence permits
>
> (91)

sexuality is viewed as something that is organic and divine, as Whit-man in "Song of Myself" wrote,

> Urge and urge and urge,
> Always the procreant urge of the world.
>
> Out of the dimness opposite equals advance,
>   always substance and increase, always sex,
> Always a knit of identity, always distinction,
>   always a breed of life.
>
> (*Complete Poetry* 26)

Another haiku by Kerouac,

> Waiting for the leaves
>   to fall;—
> There goes one!
>
> (*Book of Haikus* 32)

not only illustrates an organic phenomenon, but captures a moment of change in nature. In the following haiku,

> No telegram today
> —Only more
> Leaves fell
>
> (5)

juxtaposing humanity to nature, Kerouac observes that nature is far more organic and far less isolated than humanity.

Several of Kerouac's haiku reflect a Confucian perspective that all things in the universe are related and united:

> The tree looks
> like a dog
> Barking at Heaven
>
> (3)

Not only does this piece show the relatedness of a tree, a dog, and Heaven, it intimates the sense that the dog and the tree, the animate and the inanimate, are united. This haiku recalls an illusion expressed in Moritake's haiku, which Ezra Pound quoted in his "Vorticism" essay:[4]

> The fallen blossom flies back to its branch:
> A butterfly
>
> ("Vorticism" 467)

Another haiku by Kerouac on the same subject,

> Shooting star!—no,
> lightning bug!—
> ah well, June night
>
> (*Book of Haikus* 151)

also depicts an illusion, as does Kerouac's "The Tree Looks" above, both haiku illustrating the Confucian thought that all things in the universe are related.

Some other haiku convey the conflated vision of Confucianism and Buddhism that all the living on earth are related and united:

Frozen
     in the birdbath,
A leaf

(5)

This piece conveys the Buddhist doctrine that all things, even the inanimate, have the Buddha nature. The reason for Kerouac's stronger attraction to Buddhism than to Christianity was his realization that Buddhists believed in the existence and transmigration of the soul in animals as well as in human beings as Christians did not.[5] Not only are the bird and a leaf in this haiku, "Frozen," related, water and ice unite them as if their souls transmigrate between them.

Still other haiku, while illustrating the Confucian and Buddhist perspective of the world that the animate and the inanimate are united, express irony and humor:

After the shower,
     among the drenched roses,
The bird thrashing in the bath

(14)

In "After the Shower," while the roses are benefiting from rainwater, the bird, thrashing in the water, appears uncomfortable. But from a human point of view, the bird also is benefiting from the rainwater, which cleans it as if the bird were taking a bath. In the following piece,

Bee, why are you
     staring at me?
I'm not a flower!

(15)

Kerouac is expressing the bee's perspective: a flower and a human being are the same, the difference being that a flower might provide a bee with honey, whereas a human being might be the bee's enemy. Another piece on the same topic,

Ignoring my bread,
     The bird peeking
In the grass

(24)

expresses irony, for seeds in the grass for the bird are far more delicious than bread, a representation of human products. Another similar haiku,

> Looking for my cat
>   in the weeds,
> I found a butterfly

(40)

is ironic and humorous, because humans unexpectedly discover beautiful things in the ugly. The perspectives of nature and humanity differ, those of beauty in particular.

Like Thoreau, Kerouac lived in close contact with nature throughout his career. He seldom stayed home for a long period of time, except for writing. He took every opportunity to practice Buddhist meditation in open fields and on high mountains. Mahayana Buddhism taught him that all things, even the inanimate, possess the Buddha nature. In *Haiku: Eastern Culture*, Blyth observed, "The scale of beings in the Buddhist universe puts man midway. The primitive animistic ideas of Japanese fall in with Buddhist system, and all are united by the theory of transmigration" (19). The hours of study and meditation Kerouac spent became a reaffirmation of his belief in and compassion for all beings. In *The Dharma Bums* he wrote, "I *know* I'm empty, awake, and that there's no difference between me and anything else. In other words it means that I've become the same as everything else. It means I've become a Buddha." Then he said, "I felt great compassion for the trees because we were the same thing; I petted the dogs who didn't argue with me ever. All dogs love God. They're wiser than their masters. I told that to the dogs, too, they listened to me perking up their ears and licking my face. They didn't care one way or the other as long as I was there" (115).

Kerouac accomplished his search for Buddhahood on Mount Hozomeen as he heard thunder. All of a sudden he saw "a green and rose rainbow shafted right down into Starvation Ridge not three hundred yards away from my door, like a bolt, like a pillar: it came among steaming clouds and orange sun turmoiling.

> What is a rainbow, Lord?
>   A hoop
> For the lowly.

The rain, as he described, "hooped right into Lightning Creek, rain and snow fell simultaneous, the lake was milkwhite a mile below, it was just too crazy." At dusk he "meditated in the yellow half moon of August. Whenever I heard thunder in the mountains it was like the iron of my mother's love" (*Dharma Bums* 189–90).[6] As he descended Mount Hozomeen, he saw "on the lake rosy reflections of celestial vapor," and said, "God, I love you. . . . I have fallen in love with you, God. Take care of us all, one way or the other" (91).

Evoking the name of God, Kerouac was conflating the concept of God, with which he grew up a Christian, and the Buddhahood he now acquired through his study and meditation. He learned that Mahayana Buddhism puts more emphasis on compassion and love than does Confucianism. For Kerouac, the doctrine that all things in the universe have the Buddha nature distinguished Buddhism from Confucianism as well as from Christianity. The concept of Buddhahood thus inspired him to love and have compassion for all things, the animate and the inanimate, the human and the subhuman.[7] In several of his haiku, he directly expressed his achievement of Buddhahood:

> I close my eyes—
>   I hear & see
> Mandala

(85)

"I Close My Eyes" envisions the self in an image of Mandala, a Buddhistic divinity. Another piece on Buddha, "The Mountains" (86), depicts an image of Buddha in terms of nature rather than a figure. In another haiku, "While Meditating" (97), Buddha is defined as a concept; a meditation yields such a concept. Kerouac is illustrating the Buddhist enlightenment by which to reach a state of mind in which one has effaced subjectivity and attained satori.

From time to time Kerouac indirectly portrays in his haiku the attainment of satori, for example,

> Quietly pouring coffee
>   in the afternoon,
> How pleasant!

(47)

Such a haiku expresses comfort and peace of mind that derive from the tranquility of one's environment. The haiku "Hot Coffee" conveys a similar sentiment:

Hot coffee
    and a cigarette—
Why zazen?

(88)

In contrast to the previous haiku, this one can be read as an argument against drinking coffee and smoking. Kerouac wondered if drinking coffee and smoking a cigarette might prevent the mind from attaining satori. He thus questioned why *zazen*, a practice of Zen, would result in the attainment of satori. The argument against drinking and smoking is reminiscent of Thoreau's admonition against such activities.[8]

Kerouac's love and compassion was extended to the nonhuman livings, as shown in some of his best haiku:

In my medicine cabinet
    the winter fly
Has died of old age

(12)

A bird on
    the branch out there
—I waved

(33)

In the first piece, "In My Medicine Cabinet," humanity is pitted against nature. It is ironic that as medicine helps humans, it does not help flies. Not only does this haiku express sympathy for the death of a fly that people would not like to see in their home, but it also suggests that the fly would have died peacefully outdoors. "A Bird on," on the other hand, not only expresses the feeling of love and friendship a person has for a bird, but it also captures a moment of affinity between the two livings, the unity of humanity and nature.

In the following haiku, Kerouac demonstrates the Buddhist doctrine of mercy and compassion in contrast to Christianity:

Shall I say no?
    —fly rubbing
its back legs

(78)

This piece suggests that Kerouac composed it in praise of Issa's famous haiku on a fly:

> You dare not strike him!
> The fly is praying with hands
> And with legs.

In this haiku by Kerouac,

> Shall I break God's commandment?
> Little fly
> Rubbing its back legs

(109)

by invoking God's Commandment in the second haiku, he is conflating the Christian doctrine with the Buddhist doctrine of mercy, which the first haiku "Shall I Say No?" expresses. In the following piece on the same subject,

> Woke up groaning
> with a dream of a priest
> Eating chicken necks

(31)

the poet betrays a nightmare a Christian-converted Buddhist would have. This haiku suggests Kerouac's view of Christians' cruelty to animals in contrast to Buddhists' belief in the existence of soul in animals.

Not only was Kerouac influenced by Mahayana Buddhism, especially its doctrine of Buddhahood and mercy, but he also became interested in Zen Buddhism as he discussed its philosophy and practice with Gary Snyder, who studied Zen in Japanese monasteries. In *Nozarashi Kiko* (*A Travel Account of My Exposure in the Fields*), Basho, a Zen Buddhist, wrote, "When I set out on my journey of a thousand leagues I packed no provisions for the road. I clung to the staff of that pilgrim of old who, it is said, 'entered the realm of nothingness under the moon after midnight'" (Keene 81). Several of Kerouac's haiku depict "the realm of nothingness":

> Everywhere beyond
> the Truth,
> Empty space blue

(86)

"Everywhere Beyond" is reminiscent of the empty space the white-ness of the whale symbolizes in Melville's *Moby-Dick*.[9] Another piece on the Zen state of mind

> Spring day—
> > in my mind
> Nothing

(124)

bears a resemblance to Richard Wright's haiku:

> It is September,
> The month in which I was born;
> And I have no thoughts.

(Wright, *Haiku* 127)

To enter the state of nothingness, one must annihilate oneself. The undisciplined self is often misguided by egotism. In Zen, one's self-reliance precludes the attainment of satori, because one's conscious-ness of self means that one is not completely free of one's thoughts and feelings and has not identified self with the absolute. Whereas in Mahayana Buddhism, as practiced in the Jodo sect in Japan, one can achieve one's salvation by praying to the Buddha, Zen Buddhism, as practiced in the Rinzai sect, urges its followers even to "kill the Bud-dha" for them to attain their enlightenment. Some of Kerouac's haiku convey Rinzai's admonition:

> There's no Buddha
> > because
> There's no me

(*Book of Haikus* 75)

> I called Hanshan
> > in the mountains
> —there was no answer

(93)

All these haiku express the Zen discipline of mind that the ultimate truth lies not in self or another person, or even a divine figure such as Buddha and Christ. The ultimate truth emerges in the state of

nothingness—nature itself. Shiki, a nineteenth-century Japanese haiku
poet, expressed a similar point of view in this haiku:

> The wind in autumn
> As for me, there are no gods,
> There are no Buddhas.

As the following haiku by Kerouac show, effacing the subject, the
suppression of egotism, is expressed indirectly:

> The trees are putting on
>   Noh plays—
> Booming, roaring

(125)

"The Trees Are Putting On" is a portrayal of nature that has nothing
to do with the subject who is watching the trees. At the same time,
the trees are likened to *noh* plays, which enact the Zen doctrine that
one must suppress egotism and subjectivity. Another piece on the Zen
discipline of mind

> The train speeding
>   thru emptiness
> —I was a trainman

(125)

describes the subject, a train speeding emptiness, a space that constitutes the realm of nothingness. The subject, which is infinitesimal and
is pitted against a vast space, cannot claim its place in it. Another haiku
on the absence of human subjectivity

> Lay the pencil
>   away—no more
> thoughts, no lead

(139)

concerns the state of nothingness, where human thoughts cannot
enter.

Still some other haiku intimate that human subjectivity is irrelevant
and suspect:

I said a joke
        under the stars
—No laughter

(39)

"You'd Be Surprised" (65), like "I Said a Joke," is a haiku that under-mines knowledge and that knowledge originates in nature. Both haiku illustrate the human mind, subjectivity, is negligible as opposed to nature, objectivity. In another haiku, "Take up a Cup of Water" (66), Kerouac tries to prove how small and irrelevant an individual is in the midst of an ocean. Another haiku on the same subject, "Or, Walking the Same or Different" (66), not only demonstrates the primacy of nature over humanity but also describes how human action is dic-tated by universal law: human existence is as ephemeral as nature is ubiquitous.

As a Beat writer, Kerouac was inspired by the Zen doctrine that to attain enlightenment is to reach the state of nothingness. Not only is this state of mind free of human subjectivity and egotism, but it is even free of religious conception. The Rinzai Zen, as noted earlier, teaches its followers that if they see Buddha in their meditations, they must "kill" him. At the same time, Kerouac was deeply influenced by Mahayana Buddhism, which teaches that one can achieve Bud-dhahood in life or death and that the human soul, buttressed by the virtues of mercy and compassion, transmigrates from one living to another.

In *The Dharma Bums*, Gary Snyder, a Zen Buddhist, had a dia-logue with Kerouac, a Mahayana Buddhist, that revealed the two different religiosities the two branches of Buddhism represented. Snyder said to Kerouac, "I appreciate your sadness about the world. 'Tis indeed. Look at that party the other night. Everybody wanted to have a good time and tried real hard but we all woke up the next day feeling sorta sad and separate. What do you think about death . . . ?" Kerouac responded, "I think death is our reward. When we die we go straight to nirvana Heaven and that's that" (159). In "On the Beat Generation," an unpublished scroll manuscript, Kerouac wrote, "Beat Generation means a generation passed over into eternity. . . . The last trembling of a leaf, at being one with all time, a sudden bril-liance of redness in the fall. . . . The beat generation knows all about haikus" (*Book of Haikus* 127). Kerouac's observations of the Beat Generation suggest that the Beat poetics is not to describe the life of the beaten but to celebrate the life of the beatific. For Kerouac, and for the Beat generation, the state of beatitude can be attained in life or death. This haiku

> The bottoms of my shoes
> are clean
> From walking in the rain

(8)

suggests that, ironically, nature, which is organic, is cleaner than humanity, which is less organic. Likewise, another haiku on the same topic, "In Back of the Supermarket" (18), ironically suggesting the supremacy of nature over humanity, contains an image of natural beauty in an unnatural environment. In "Glow Worms" (137), Kerouac is envious of the glow worms sleeping on his flowers, which are oblivious of the chaotic society of which he is a member. This haiku has an affinity with Frost's "After Apple-Picking," in which Frost is as envious of the woodchuck's peaceful hibernation as he is afraid of a nightmare caused by the chaotic world.[10] In this haiku by Kerouac,

> Am I a flower
> bee, that you
> Stare at me?

(155)

Kerouac is flattered: to the bee he looks as attractive as a flower, an image of beatitude.

Wandering in the fields and the woods, as Kerouac describes in *The Dharma Bums*, he thought that "the substance of my bones and their bones and the bones of dead men in the earth of rain at night is the common individual substance that is everlastingly tranquil and blissful?" A thought occurred to him: "Raindrops are ecstasy, raindrops are not different from ecstasy, neither is ecstasy different from raindrops, yea, ecstasy is raindrops, rain on, O cloud!" (110). Many of the haiku collected in his notebooks, "V. 1958–1959: Beat Generation Haikus / Autumn," and "VI. 1960–1966: Northport Haikus / Winter," describe what he called "ecstasy":

> The droopy constellation
> on the grassy hill—
> Emily Dickinson's Tomb

(154)

> In enormous blizzard
>   burying everything
> My cat's out mating

> (164)

Because the aim of a Beat poet is to reach eternity, the first haiku, "The Droopy Constellation," is reminiscent of Emily Dickinson's poetry. In such poems as "I Died for Beauty" and "Because I Could Not Stop for Death," Dickinson describes her journey to eternity.[11] In the second haiku, "In Enormous Blizzard," an image of a powerful blizzard burying everything on earth suggests death and eternity, but it is juxtaposed to an image of love-making that suggest life and ecstasy. This piece bears a resemblance to Basho's "The Love of the Cats":

> The love of the cats;
> When it was over, the hazy moon
>   Over the bed-chamber.

> (Blyth, *Haiku* 264)

Both of Kerouac's haiku suggest there is ecstasy in life and death, love and eternity.

Kerouac's Beat poetics, based on Zen doctrine, led to his concept of individual freedom. Lying on his bag smoking, as Kerouac describes his experience in *The Dharma Bums*, he thought, "Everything is possible. I am God, I am Buddha, I am imperfect Ray Smith, all at the same time, I am empty space, I am all things. I have all the time in the world from life to life to do what is to do, to do what is done, to do the timeless doing, infinitely perfect within, why cry, why worry, perfect like mind essence and the minds of banana peels" (97). Later, envisioning "the bliss of the Buddha-fields," he wrote, "I saw that my life was a vast glowing empty page and I could do anything I wanted" (117). Earlier in the novel, he also recounts the life of a truck driver who gave him a ride when he was hitchhiking to visit his mother in North Carolina. He found that the driver "had a nice home in Ohio with wife, daughter, Christmas tree, two cars, garage, lawn, lawnmower, but he couldn't enjoy any of it because he really wasn't free" (102).

In his notebook collection, "Beat Generation Haikus, 1958–1959," Kerouac included the following piece, which deals with individual freedom:

> Jack reads his book
> aloud at nite
> —the stars come out.

> (*Book of Haikus* 133)

This haiku challenges the Zen concept of *mu* and asserts human sub-jectivity. Declaring his own ideas, Kerouac is able to find his audience. His call and the stars' response suggest that his vision of the world is as objective as the world's vision of him is subjective. Such a haiku is reminiscent of Robert Frost's poem "The Road Not Taken."[12] Like Frost, Kerouac takes pride in being free and being a nonconformist. Kerouac's haiku, such as "On Desolation / I was the alonest man / in the world" (136) and "High noon / in Northport / —Alien shore" (137) also reflect individual freedom and autonomy. "On Desolation" and "High Noon" both cherish Kerouac's state of mind dictated by no one but himself. To him, alienation from a corrupt society will lead him to nirvana. Both haiku recall Langston Hughes's "The Weary Blues," in which a blues musician takes pride in his alienation and autonomy.[13] The following piece, "Reading the Sutra," recounts that the Buddhist scripture inspired Kerouac to attain enlightenment by decisive action on his part:

> Reading the sutra
> I decided
> To go straight

> (143)

This haiku has an affinity with Gwendolyn Brooks's "We Real Cool," in which the African American pool players are portrayed as daring individuals who enjoyed living freely on their instincts as did the beatniks.[14]

Not only are Kerouac's Beat Generation haiku poignant expres-sions of freedom and individualism, many of them can be read as direct indictments against materialistic society. Such haiku as "Perfect moonlit night / marred / By family squabble" (17) and "A quiet Autumn night / and these fools / Are starting to argue" (177) thrive on the images of celestial beauty. The image of the universe in har-mony, however, is juxtaposed to the image of society in conflict. Such a haiku above is in contrast to another Beat Generation haiku by Kerouac:

        Ah, the crickets
                are screaming
        at the moon

                                        (140)

In this piece the crickets, as they scream at the moon, the preeminent
object in the sky, do not quarrel among themselves. This haiku suggests that human beings, by contrast, at times scream to one another
rather than talk about beautiful things on earth and in the sky. In the
following haiku

        Desk cluttered
                with mail—
        My mind is quiet

                                        (145)

Kerouac is able to attain his peace of mind, despite the image of a clut-
tered desk representing a chaotic society in which the Beat poet lives.
    In sum, Kerouac early in his career was well versed in the writings
of American transcendentalists, such as Emerson, Thoreau, and Whitman, as well as in Emily Dickinson's poetry. He also found American
transcendentalists well acquainted with Confucianism and Buddhism.
Through his friendship with such Beat poets as Allen Ginsberg and
Gary Snyder, as well as through his studies of Buddhism, Zen, and
R. H. Blyth's volume, *Haiku: Eastern Culture* in particular, Kerouac
firmly established his poetics. The numerous haiku he wrote reflect his
fascination with Mahayana Buddhism, as well as with Zen philosophy.
What is remarkable about his haiku is that not only was he influenced
by the books he read, but he was also inspired by his own experience
in wandering and meditating in the fields and on the mountains.

CHAPTER 7

RICHARD WRIGHT'S HAIKU, ZEN, AND THE AFRICAN "PRIMAL OUTLOOK UPON LIFE"

Richard Wright is acclaimed for his powerful prose in *Native Son* (1940) and *Black Boy* (1945), books that he wrote early in his career. But later in his life he became interested in poetry, especially the haiku. In the 1950s he liked to work in the garden on his Normandy farm, an activity that supplied many themes for his haiku (Fabre, *Unfinished Quest* 447). Of Wright's other experiences in this period, his travels to the newly independent Ghana in West Africa are also reflected in his haiku. The African philosophy of life Wright witnessed among the Ashanti, the "primal outlook upon life," as he called it, served as an inspiration for his poetic sensibility (*Black Power* 266)

By the spring of 1960, Wright informed his friend and Dutch translator Margrit de Sablonière that he had returned to poetry and added, "During my illness I experimented with the Japanese form of poetry called haiku; I wrote some 4,000 of them and am now sifting them out to see if they are any good." In his discussion of this development, Michel Fabre notes that Wright's interest in haiku involved research into the great Japanese masters, Basho, Buson, and Issa; he ignored the European and American forms that were then becoming popular. Fabre states further that "Wright made an effort to respect the exact form of the poem" but adds that it was curious for Wright to become interested in haiku at a time when he was fighting illness. As Fabre reasons, "Logically he should have been tempted to turn away from 'pure' literature and to use his pen instead as a weapon" (*Unfinished Quest* 505–6).

Constance Webb says that Wright had lost his physical energy and that "while lying against the pillows one afternoon he picked up the small book of Japanese poetry and began to read it again" (Webb 393). Apparently, Wright had borrowed it from a friend, a South African poet.[1] Wright read and reread the classic haiku collected in the book. Webb comments that Wright "had to study it and study to find out why it struck his ear with such a modern note" (Webb 387). The haiku "seemed to answer the rawness he felt, which had, in turn, created a sensitivity that ached. Never had he been so sensitive, as if his nervous system had been exposed to rough air" (Webb 393). In a letter to Paul Reynolds, his friend and literary agent, Wright explained that he had sent to William Targ of the World Publishing Company an eighty-two-page manuscript of haiku titled *This Other World: Projections in the Haiku Manner*. After a few comments about Targ, Wright went on to say, "These poems are the results of my being in bed a great deal and it is likely that they are bad. I don't know" (Webb 394).

That manuscript had not been published in its entirety until 1998.[2] We will never fully know the reasons why Wright turned to haiku during the last years of his life, but a reading of the haiku in *This Other World*, as well as the rest of his haiku, indicates that Wright turned away from the moral, intellectual, social, and political problems dealt with in his prose work and found in nature his latent poetic sensibility. Gwendolyn Brooks called Wright's haiku collected in *This Other World* "a clutch of strong flowers."[3] Wright's daughter remarks in her introduction to the volume, "These haiku not only helped him place the volcanic experience of mourning under the self-control of closely counted syllables, but also enabled him to come to terms with the difficult beauty of the earth in which his mother would be laid to rest."[4] Wright's discovery of haiku, as Fabre says, "brings to light an often neglected aspect of the writer's personality: his intimate sense of the universal harmony, his wonder before life, his thirst for a natural existence, all these tendencies which nourished, as much as did any ideology or faith, his courageous and incessant battle against all that prevents an individual from fully belonging to the world" ("Poetry of Wright" 271).

The genesis of Wright's poetic sensibility can be glimpsed in his "Blueprint for Negro Writing," even though its theory is Marxist. An African American writer's perspective, Wright states, "is that part of a poem, novel, or play which a writer never puts directly upon paper. It is that fixed point in intellectual space where a writer stands to view the struggles, hopes, and sufferings of his people" ("Blueprint" 45). Wright establishes this vantage point in the autobiographical prose of *Black Boy*, yet he also consciously creates there a poetic vision of nature through and against which racial conflict is depicted. The poetic passages in *Black Boy* demonstrate Wright's incipient interest in the exaltation of nature and show the congeniality of images from nature to his sensibility.

On the basis of J. B. Danquah's *The Akan Doctrine of God*, Wright was persuaded of the African belief that spirits reside in inanimate objects like trees, stones, and rivers. Wright also adopted an African belief in ghosts and in the spirits of the dead, which meant that life and death are not diametrically opposed. "Life in the ghost world," he remarks, "is an exact duplicate of life in this world. A farmer in this world is a farmer there; a chief here is a chief there. It is, therefore, of decisive importance when one enters that world of ghostly shades to enter it in the right manner. For you can be snubbed there just as effectively and humiliatingly as you were snubbed here" (*Black Power* 214). This African religion furthermore does not recognize the existence of hell and sin, nor does it distinguish in the abstract between good and evil. "When the family is the chief idea," Wright quotes Danquah as saying, "things that are dishonorable and undignified, actions that in disgracing you disgrace the family, are held to be vices, and the highest virtue is found in honor and dignity. Tradition is the determinant of what is right and just, what is good and done." Whereas the Akan religion and Christianity share the concept of life after death, the Akan religion also resembles other religions such as Buddhism and Hinduism in its belief in reincarnation. Unlike Christianity, the Akan religion, as do Buddhism and Hinduism, believes in the existence of soul in nonhuman beings. "Death," Wright observes, "does not round off life; it is not the end; it complements life." To him the African religion looks "terrifying" but not "primitive" (*Black Power* 215–17)

One of the theoretical principles in "Blueprint" calls for African American writers to explore universal humanism, what is common among all cultures. "Every iota of gain in human thought and sensibility," Wright argues, "should be ready grist for his mill, no matter how far-fetched they may seem in their immediate implications" ("Blueprint" 45). After a journey into the Ashanti kingdom in West Africa in 1953, when he was forty-five, Wright asserted in *Black Power*, "The truth is that the question of how much of Africa has survived in the New World is misnamed when termed 'African survivals.' The African attitude toward life springs from a natural and poetic grasp of existence and all the emotional implications that such an attitude carries; it is clear, then, that what the anthropologists have been trying to explain are not 'African survivals' at all—they are but the retention of basic and primal attitudes toward life" (*Black Power* 266). Wright's exploration of the Ashanti convinced him that the defense of African culture meant renewal of Africans' faith in themselves. He came to see African culture buttressed by traditional human values—awe of nature, family kinship and love, the sense of honor—that had made the African survivals possible.

When an African was transplanted to Europe or America, as Wright observed, that person identified himself or herself with the rational, urban, and economic way of life in the West but retained his or her traditional values. In particular, the transplanted African kept intact the awe of nature. That person, Wright argued, "remains black and becomes American, English, or French" but "to the degree that he fails to adjust, to absorb the new environment (and this will be mainly for racial and economic reasons!), he, to that degree, and of necessity, will retain much of his primal outlook upon life, his basically poetic apprehension of existence." The way in which the African sees nature, as Wright realized, is humanistic and is not materialistic. "The tribal African's culture," Wright argued, "*is* primally human; that which *all* men once had as their warm, indigenous way of living, is his. . . . There is nothing mystical or biological about it. When one realizes that one is dealing with two distinct and separate worlds of psychological being, two conceptions of time even, the problem becomes clear; it is a clash between two systems of culture" (*Black Power* 266).

If the African American, such as Wright himself, retained, in time or for a time, this "primal" outlook on life, it was because that person was unable to "see or feel or trust (at that moment in history) any other system of value or belief": "What the social scientist should seek for are not 'African survivals' at all, but the persistence and vitality of primal attitudes and the social causes thereof. And he would discover that the same primal attitudes exist among other people; after all, what are the basic promptings of artists, poets, and actors but primal attitudes consciously held?" (*Black Power* 267). When Wright studied R. H. Blyth's four volumes on the art and history of haiku,[5] he was struck with a strong affinity between the worldview that underlies haiku and the African "primal outlook upon life" that buttresses Ashanti culture, one of the oldest in Africa. Unlike Western romantic poetry and even the earlier Japanese poetry called *waka*, Blyth observes that haiku "is as near to life and nature as possible, as far from literature and fine writing as may be, so that the asceticism is art and the art is asceticism" (*History* 1: 1). Blyth's definition of haiku as an ascetic art means that the classic haiku by such masters as Basho, Buson, and Issa that Wright emulated, strictly concern objects and phenomena in nature.

In composing a haiku, the poet must, at first, observe an object or phenomenon in nature from a perspective devoid of thoughts and feelings. Only after the poet attains that stance and vision will the poet be able to achieve a harmonious union with nature.

The haiku poet's perspective without egotism bears a strong resemblance to the African's view of nature and self. In African life, Wright saw a closer relationship between human beings and nature than that between human beings and their social and political environment: "Africa, with its high rain forest, with its stifling heat and lush vegetation, might well be mankind's queerest laboratory. Here instinct ruled and flowered without being concerned with the nature of the physical structure of the world; man lived without too much effort; there was nothing to distract him from concentrating upon the currents and countercurrents of his heart. He was thus free to project out of himself what he thought he was. Man has lived here in a waking dream, and, to some extent, he still lives here in that dream." Africa evokes in one "a total attitude toward life, calling into question the basic assumptions of existence" (*Black Power* 159). Wright was moreover fascinated by the African reverence for the nonhuman living, a primal attitude that corresponds to the haiku poet's awe of nature. He thus observed, "The pre-Christian African was impressed with the littleness of himself and he walked the earth warily, lest he disturb the presence of invisible gods. When he wanted to disrupt the terrible majesty of the ocean in order to fish, he first made sacrifices to its crashing and rolling waves; he dared not cut down a tree without first propitiating its spirit so that it would not haunt him; he loved his fragile life and he was convinced that the tree loved its life also" (*Black Power* 261–62). For Wright, not only do the African and the haiku poet share an intuitive, selfless worldview, but they also have the common belief that humankind does not occupy the central place in the world.

In studying Blyth's analysis and reading of classic haiku, Wright learned that haiku masters were able to present in direct statement the paradox of union with nature, expressing the desire to be a part of nature while simultaneously maintaining their separate identity. Born and trained in Western culture and tradition, Wright as an artist must have struggled to develop such a characteristic in his haiku. Classic haiku call for simplicity of language, thought, and image, a lack of complication often revealed in the spontaneous joy of union with nature. The joy, Blyth points out, comes from "the (apparent) re-union of ourselves with things," our being among others (*Haiku* 9). Austerity on the part of the poet is not only a lack of intellectualization; it is almost a wordlessness, a condition in which words are used not to externalize the poet's state of feeling, but to "clear away something that seems to stand between" the poet and things in the world. Because things in the world are not actually separate from the poet, they "are then perceived by self-knowledge" (*Haiku* 176). Classic haiku, as Wright learned, remove as many words as possible, stressing nonintellectuality, for thought must depend on and not substitute for intuition.

Another major characteristic of haiku that Wright learned is a love of nature that is inseparable from the ordinary. For Blyth this characteristic is explained in terms of selflessness, meaning that the poet has identified with nature. The loss of the poet's individuality involves a generalized melancholy or loneliness as an underlying rhythm. It represents the state of Zen, of "absolute spiritual poverty in which, having nothing, we possess all" (*Haiku* 162). In Zen-inspired haiku, the material or the concrete is emphasized without the expression of any general principles of abstract reasoning. Animate and inanimate lose their differences, so that one might say haiku are not about human beings but about things. Zen teaches, as Blyth observes, that the ordinary thing and the love of nature are reduced to a detached love of life as it is, without idealistic, moralistic, or ethical attachments. Things are equal to human beings; both exist through and because of each other.

Directly concerned with objects and phenomena in nature, a classic haiku poet like Basho completely suppressed subjectivity. So did Jack Kerouac, as noted earlier, in many of the haiku he was inspired to write by the state of Zen. Wright also attempted to do so as much as possible in many of his haiku. His interest in this doctrine in Zen, the effacement of subjectivity, is reflected in his haiku numbered 508:

508.   It is September
        The month in which I was born;
          And I have no thoughts.

In the first haiku in *Haiku: This Other World*, Wright, as the subject as well as the narrator, describes himself deprived of his name and of his subjectivity:

1.   I am nobody:
        A red sinking autumn sun
          Took my name away.

The wood in the following haiku is not an ordinary scene; it now exists with different meaning:

809.   Why did this spring wood
            Grow so silent when I came?
                What was happening?

In the next haiku, Wright tries to suppress egotism and attain a state of nothingness:

721.   As my anger ebbs,
        The spring stars grow bright again
            And the wind returns.

As he relieves himself of anger, he begins to see the stars "grow bright again" and "the wind" return. Only when he reaches a state of nothingness is he able to perceive nature with his enlightened senses.

In some of his haiku, as the following examples show, Wright offers simple scenes in which human beings and nature exist in harmony, in contrast to complex, intriguing scenes in society where people are at strife.

42.   Seen from a hilltop,
        Shadowy in winter rain,
            A man and his mule.

377.   In the winter dusk,
        A thin girl leads a black cow
            By a dragging rope.

541.   After the sermon,
        The preacher's voice is still heard
            In the caws of crows.

"Seen from a Hilltop" (42) finds unity in humankind and nature: a man, a mule, a rain, a meadow, and a hill. "In the Winter Dusk" (377), like "Seen from a Hilltop" (42), is a direct description of the scene where a girl lives in harmony with an animal. It is not clear whether a girl leads a cow or the cow her. Since the rope is dragging, neither the girl nor the cow is forcing the other to move. Creating such an ambiguous image intensifies the unity and harmony between the living. In "After the Sermon" (541), the seasonal reference is ambiguous, but Wright finds a continuity between humanity and nature, "the preacher's voice" and "the caws of crows."[6]

Whether perceiving nature for its own sake or in its relation to humankind, Wright's haiku thrive on the subtle interactions among the senses captured in seventeen syllables. For instance, in number 47, the poet seems to detach himself from a natural scene:

> 47.   The spring lingers on
> In the scent of a damp log
>   Rotting in the sun.

The feeling of the warm sun, the scent of a damp log, the sight and silence of an outdoor scene, all coalesce into an image of spring. In the process the overall image has evolved from the separate images of the sun, the log, and the atmosphere. The images of sight, moreover, are intertwined with the images of warmth from the sun and the rotting log as well as with the image of smell from the log, all these images interacting with one another. In trying his hand at haiku, Wright initially modeled his on those of the classic Japanese poets such as Moritake, Basho, Kikaku, Buson, and Issa. Two of the haiku in *This Other World* have a thematic resemblance to a famous haiku by Moritake, "The fallen blossom flies back to its branch: / A butterfly" (Pound, "Vorticism" 467):

> 626.   Off the cherry tree,
> One twig and its red blossom
>   Flies into the sun.

> 669.   A leaf chases wind
> Across an autumn river
>   And shakes a pine tree.

Both of Wright's haiku "Off the Cherry Tree" (626) and "A Leaf Chases Wind" (669) create an illusion similar to that in Moritake's haiku. In "Off the Cherry Tree," a twig with its red blossom flies into the sun as if a bird flew off the cherry tree. Likewise, "A Leaf Chases Wind" captures a scene as though a leaf were chasing wind and shaking a pine tree rather than the other way around.

According to Margaret Walker, Wright was fascinated by American modernist poets, including Pound. "In the last years of his life," she notes, "Wright discovered the Japanese form of poetry known as Haiku and became more than a little interested in what was not just a strange and foreign stanza but an exercise in conciseness—getting so much meaning or philosophy in so few words" (*Richard Wright* 313–14). Pound's theory that the poet's use of an image is not to support "some system of ethics or economics" coincides with a theory that haiku express the poet's intuitive worldview. Wright, then, found the haiku poet's intuitive worldview akin to that of the African. Because both views have little to do with politics or economics directly, Wright's haiku remain a radical departure from his earlier work in prose.

Whether Wright was influenced by Pound's imagism is difficult to determine, but many of Wright's haiku bear a close resemblance to classic Japanese haiku. In both style and content, a pair of his haiku in *This Other World* are reminiscent of two of Basho's most celebrated haiku. Wright's "In the Silent Forest" echoes Basho's "How Quiet It Is!":

316.   In the silent forest
       A woodpecker hammers at
            The sound of silence.

            How quiet it is!
       Piercing into the rocks
            The cicada's voice.[7]

As Basho expresses awe at quiet, Wright juxtaposes silence in the forest to the sound of a woodpecker. Similarly, Wright's "A Thin Waterfall" is akin to Basho's "A Crow":

569.   A thin waterfall
       Dribbles the whole autumn night,—
            How lonely it is.

            A crow
       Perched on a withered tree
            In the autumn evening.[8]

Basho focuses on a single crow perching on a branch of an old tree, as does Wright on a thin waterfall. In both haiku, the scene is drawn with little detail and the mood is provided by a simple, reserved description of fact, a phenomenon in nature. In both haiku, parts of the scene are painted in dark colors, as is the background. Both haiku create the kind of beauty associated with the aesthetic sensibility of *sabi* that suggests loneliness and quietude, the salient characteristics of nature, as opposed to overexcitement and loudness, those of society.[9] As Basho expresses *sabi* with the image of autumn evening, so does Wright with the line "How lonely it is," a subjective perception. The two haiku, however, are different: while Basho describes nature for its own sake, Wright interjects his own feelings in his description. Whether Wright and Basho actually felt lonely when writing the haiku is moot.

Legend has it that Basho inspired more disciples than did any other haiku poet. Kikaku is regarded as Basho's most innovative disciple. Two of Wright's haiku bear some resemblance to Kikaku's "The Bright Harvest Moon," since both poets emphasize an interaction between humanity and nature in the creation of beauty:

> 106.   Beads of quicksilver
> On a black umbrella:
>   Moonlit April rain.

> 671.   A pale winter moon,
> Pitying a lonely doll,
>   Lent it a shadow.

> The bright harvest moon
> Upon the tatami mats
> Shadows of the pines.

> (Kikaku)[10]

In Kikaku's haiku, the beauty of the moonlight is not only humanized by the light shining on the man-made objects, but it is also intensified by the shadows of pine trees that fall on the mats. The intricate pattern of the shadow of the trees intensifies the beauty of the moonlight. Not only does such a scene unify an image of humanity and an image of nature, but it also shows that humanity and nature can interact positively. In Wright's first poem an element of nature, "beads of quicksilver," is reinforced by a manufactured object, "a black umbrella." In "A Pale Winter Moon," while the second line projects loneliness onto a doll, the beauty of the winter moon is intensified by the presence of a human-made object. In contrast to the four haiku quoted previously (Wright's "In the Silent Forest" and "A Thin Waterfall," Basho's "How Quiet It Is!" and "A Crow"), these three haiku by Wright and Kikaku do lightly include human subjectivity in appreciating natural beauty, although the focus of their visions is nature.

Wright's "I Would Like a Bell" is comparable to Buson's well-known "On the Hanging Bell" in depicting a spring scene, but Wright's poem focuses on a human subjectivity, a desiring self:

13.   I would like a bell
        Tolling in this soft twilight
              Over willow trees.

        On the hanging bell
        Has perched and is fast asleep,
        It's a butterfly.[11]

Buson was well known in his time as an accomplished painter, and many of his haiku reflect his singular attention to color and its intensification. Wright's "A Butterfly Makes," for example, is reminiscent of Buson's "Also Stepping On"; both imply a subjective perception:

82.   A butterfly makes
        The sunshine even brighter
              With fluttering wings.

        Also stepping on
        The mountain pheasant's tail is
        The spring setting sun.[12]

In another fine haiku, Wright portrays humanity's relationship with nature in terms of art:

571.   From across the lake,
        Past the black winter trees,
              Faint sounds of a flute.

Unlike "The Spring Lingers On" (47), discussed earlier, "From across the Lake" (571) admits a human involvement in the scene: someone is playing the flute as the poet is listening from the other side of the lake. Through transference of the senses between the faint sounds of a flute and the black winter trees, a positive interaction of humanity and nature takes place. "From across the Lake" has an affinity with Kikaku's "The Harvest Moon," noted earlier, for both haiku are expressions of beauty perceived by subjects in an interaction of natural and human objects.

Wright's haiku in their portrayal of humankind's association with nature often convey a kind of enlightenment, a new way of looking at human beings and nature, as in the following examples:

720.   A wilting jonquil
            Journeys to its destiny
            In a shut bedroom.

722.   Lines of winter rain
            Gleam only as they flash past
            My lighted window.

"A Wilting Jonquil" (720) teaches the poet a lesson that natural things out of context cannot exhibit their beauty. In "Lines of Winter Rain" (722), the poet learns that sometimes only when an interaction between human beings and nature occurs can natural beauty be savored.

While haiku poets often tried to suppress subjectivity in depicting nature, some of Wright's haiku bring the poet to the fore. While haiku 720, "A Wilting Jonquil," focuses on an object, haiku 722, "Lines of Winter Rain," insists on the importance of "my lighted window." None of the classic haiku Wright emulates express the poet's thoughts or feelings. The first haiku in Wright's *Haiku: This Other World* ("I am nobody: / A red sinking autumn sun / Took my name away"), as noted earlier, suppresses subjectivity by depicting the red sun that erases his name. And yet the poet is strongly present, even by negation. The same is true of some of his other haiku discussed earlier, such as haiku 809, "Why did this spring wood / Grow so silent when I came? / What was happening?" and haiku 721, "As my anger ebbs, / The spring stars grow bright again / And the wind returns."

Writing a haiku to depict a spring scene, quoted earlier, Wright and Buson take different approaches in terms of subjectivity: "I would like a bell / Tolling in this soft twilight / Over willow trees" (Wright); "On the hanging bell / Has perched and is fast asleep, / It's a butterfly" (Buson). Wright's focus is on imagining a bell ringing softly over willow trees, while Buson's is on a butterfly actually fast asleep on a hanging bell. The two haiku are quite different: subjectivity is present in Wright's haiku, whereas it is absent in Buson's. Another pair of haiku by Wright and Basho portray autumn scenes: "A thin waterfall / Dribbles the whole autumn night,— / How lonely it is" (Wright); "A crow / Perched on a withered tree / In the autumn evening" (Basho). Subjectivity is absent in Basho's haiku, whereas it is directly expressed by Wright's third line, "How lonely it is." In depicting the moon, for example, Wright and Kikaku write remarkably different haiku: "A pale winter moon, / Pitying a lonely doll, / Lent it a shadow" (Wright); "The bright harvest moon / Upon the tatami mats / Shadows of the pines" (Kikaku). Subjectivity is entirely absent in Kikaku's haiku, whereas it is strongly expressed in Wright's with the middle line, "Pitying a lonely doll."

Absent subjectivity in composing haiku is akin to Jacques Lacan's concept of the subject. Lacan, a postmodern psychoanalyst, challenged the traditional concept of subjectivity. On the basis of his analytic experience, he saw subjectivity as a concept that concerns neither the autonomy of the self nor the subject's ability to influence the other. Subjectivity is deficient because of the deficiencies inherent in language: "The effects of language are always mixed with the fact, which is the basis of the analytic experience, that the subject is subject only from being subjected to the field of the Other, the subject proceeds from his synchronic subjection in the field of the Other. That is why he must get out, get himself out, and in the *getting-himself-out*, in the end, he will know that the real Other has, just as much as himself, to get himself out, to pull himself free" (*Four Fundamental Concepts of Psychoanalysis* 188). Because the subject, an infinitesimal fraction in time and space, is isolated from the world, the subject is only capable of imagining the other: society, nature, and life. Only when the subject is conscious of the deficiencies of language, as Lacan theorized, does the subject of the unconscious emerge. Only then is the subject able to approach and encounter the truth of life—what Lacan called "the real" and "the unsymbolizable."

To Lacan, the motive for subjectivity aimed at the symbolic—what constitutes tradition, religion, law, and so on—whereas the motive for absence of subjectivity aimed at the unconscious, a state largely derived from the other and partly derived from the imaginary on the part of the subject. The unconscious, then, is closer to the real than it is to the symbolic; the imaginary is closer to the real than it is to the symbolic. Lacan posited, however, that "there exists a world of truth entirely deprived of subjectivity," universal truth, "and that . . . there has been a historical development of subjectivity manifestly directed towards the rediscovery of truth," historically subjective truth, "which lies in the order of symbols" (*Seminar* 2: 285). Lacan saw the door as language; the door is open either to the real or to the imaginary. He said that "we don't know quite which, but it is either one or the other. There is an asymmetry between the opening and the closing— if the opening of the door controls access, when closed, it closes the

circuit" (*Seminar* 2: 302). He considers language either objective or
subjective; the real is objective whereas the imaginary is subjective.
Applied to traditional haiku composition, language aims at the real
through the imaginary rather than at the symbolic through the historically subjective.

The Lacanian distinction of the imaginary and the symbolic has an
affinity with one of the disagreements between Pound and Yeats in
reading Japanese poetry and drama. Pound regarded symbolism as "a
sort of allusion, almost of allegory." The symbolists, Pound thought,
"degraded the symbol to the status of a word. . . . Moreover, one
does not want to be called a symbolist, because symbolism has usually been associated with mushy technique" ("Vorticism" 463). For
Pound, symbolism is inferior to imagism, the imaginary in Lacan's
theory, because in symbolism one image is used to suggest another
or to represent another, whereby both images would be weakened.
Pound's theory of imagism was derived from haiku, as noted earlier,
which shuns metaphor and symbolism, rather than from the *noh* play,
which Yeats considered indirect and symbolic.

In any event, Lacan moreover envisioned a domain of the real
beyond "the navel of the dream, this abyssal relation to that which
is most unknown, which is the hallmark of an exceptional, privileged
experience, in which the real is apprehended beyond all mediation,
be it imaginary or symbolic." Lacan equated this domain with "an
absolute other . . . an other beyond all intersubjectivity" (*Seminar* 2:
176–77). In Lacanian terms, the haiku poet is motivated to depict the
real directly without using symbols. In this process the poet relies on
the imaginary, a domain that is closer to nature, where subjectivity is
suppressed as much as possible or minimized. The poets avoid symbols in writing haiku in an attempt to be objective and yet creative.
"If the symbolic function functions," Lacan lamented, "we are inside
it. And I would even say—we are so far into it that we can't get out of
it" (*Seminar* 2: 31).

That symbolism is an obstacle in writing haiku can be explained
in terms of Lacan's definition of the symbolic order. Lacan observed
that language symbolizes things that do not exist, non-being: "The
fundamental relation of man to this symbolic order is very precisely
what founds the symbolic order itself—the relation of non-being
to being. . . . What insists on being satisfied can only be satisfied in
recognition. The end of the symbolic process is that non-being come
to be, because it has spoken" (*Seminar* 2: 308). To Lacan, then, language makes non-being become being. Because haiku aims to represent

being rather than non-being, what Lacan called "language" or what is "spoken" does not apply to the language of haiku.

Not only is Lacan's theory of language applicable to the unsymbolic characteristic of haiku, it clearly accounts for the absence of subjectivity in traditional haiku. Those haiku by Wright that express subjectivity directly or indirectly might be considered modern rather than traditional. The first line in Wright's haiku 13 ("I would like a bell / Tolling in this soft twilight / Over willow trees."), quoted earlier, constitutes an expression of subjectivity, but the second line, "Tolling in this soft twilight," is an image created by the imaginary. Pound's haiku-like poem "In a Station of the Metro," noted earlier, has been regarded as imagistic and modernistic: "The apparition of these faces in the crowd: / Petals, on a wet, black bough." Since the image of the apparition, as well as that of petals, as Pound explains in his "Vorticism" essay, are derived from the subject's experience at the metro station, this poem indirectly expresses subjectivity. Pound also expresses subjectivity directly in another haiku-like poem, titled "Alba":

> As cool as the pale wet leaves
> > of lily-of-the-valley
> She lay beside me in the dawn.

> (*Selected Poems* 36)

As the image of "the pale wet leaves," a creation by the imaginary in Lacanian terms, indirectly expresses the subject's desire, the last line explicitly brings in the desiring subject. One of the disciplines in classic haiku composition calls for restraining the expression of desire. "Desire" as Lacan observed, "always becomes manifest at the joint of speech, where it makes its appearance, its sudden emergence, its surge forwards. Desire emerges just as it becomes embodied in speech, it emerges with symbolism" (*Seminar* 2: 234).

As Wright's and Pound's modernist haiku demonstrate, subjectivity in such haiku is expressed through the use of a personal pronoun, and the subject's desire is evoked in an image that reflects subjectivity. Subjectivity and desire, its dominant construct, are both expressed through pronominal language rather than through an image in nature that embodies the real or the unconscious. Because Wright wrote haiku under the influences of classic Japanese haiku poets in the seventeenth and eighteenth centuries, a great majority of his haiku, perhaps eight out of ten, can be categorized as traditional haiku, in which an image of nature is the focus of the poem and subjectivity is absent.

Wright saw the images of nature he created in his haiku as expressing the "primal outlook upon life" he acquired in Africa. As he traveled to Ghana in 1953 to write *Black Power*, a postmodern and postcolonial nonfiction, he was deeply impressed with the African worldview that human beings are not at the center of the universe, a worldview that corresponds with that of Zen. Ashanti culture and belief, in particular, convinced Wright that the world of nature is preeminent over the subjective vision of that world. In writing traditionalist haiku, Wright adopted a poetic form in which subjectivity, egotism, and desire stand in the way of seeking truth. Not only do most of his haiku thrive on poignant images of nature, but also they admonish the reader that only by paying nature the utmost attention can human beings truly see themselves.

CHAPTER 8

CROSS-CULTURAL POETICS

SONIA SANCHEZ'S
LIKE THE SINGING COMING OFF THE DRUMS

Some accomplished poets produced their work in isolation. Emily Dickinson is one of the world's best-known and widely admired poets, though at the time of her death in 1886, only eight of her more than seventeen hundred poems had been published. Richard Wright, as noted earlier, wrote in exile more than four thousand haiku in his last year and half. Yet only twenty-four of them had posthumously appeared in print before the publication of *Haiku: This Other World* (1998), a collection of 817 haiku Wright himself had selected.

Times have changed, not only for the poet but also for the literary public. Readers of poetry over a century ago were not quite familiar with the style and vision of Dickinson, who wrote those terse verses with their bold, startling imagery, nor were they as interested in cross-cultural visions as are today's readers. When Wright experimented with those massive haiku in the late 1950s, he did so in isolation, just as Dickinson wrote her poems. Recovering from illness, Wright composed his haiku in bed at home as well as in the hospital, in cafés, in restaurants, and in Paris as well as in the French countryside.

Sonia Sanchez, by contrast, has appeared as a postmodern, postcolonial, and remarkably cross-cultural poet. Such an observation, however, does not suggest that Dickinson and Wright were less cross-cultural. Indeed, Dickinson's readers have long recognized in her poetry the Calvinist tendency to look inwardly, as well as the transcendental view of nature and humanity. Many of her poems also exhibit a dialogue she had with contemporary industrial culture. And Wright's later work, such as "The Man Who Lived Underground" and haiku, shows his interest in French existentialism as well as in Zen aesthetics.

While Sanchez is known as an activist poet, much of her poetic impulse in *Like the Singing Coming off the Drums* (1998) derives from the tradition of Japanese haiku, in which a poet pays the utmost attention to the beauty inherent in nature. A great majority of Sanchez's latest collection of poems are titled haiku, tanka, or sonku. Reading such poems indicates that Sanchez, turning away from the moral, intellectual, social, and political problems dealt with in her other work, found in nature her latent poetic sensibility. Above all, her fine pieces of poetry show, as do classic Japanese haiku and *tanka* (short song), the unity and harmony of all things, the sensibility that nature and humanity are one and inseparable. In this collection, much of her poetry poignantly expresses a desire to transcend social and racial differences and a need to find union and harmony with nature.

1

Many of the haiku and *tanka* presented in the first section of Sanchez's collection, titled "Naked in the Streets," reflects the poetic tradition in which human action emulates nature. As the section title suggests, Sanchez creates an image of nature out of a scene of streets. Today the poet as well as most of her readers live in urban communities in close contact with the streets, just as classic haiku poets and their readers lived and worked closely with nature. The first haiku in *Like the Singing Coming off the Drums* conveys a delightful sensation one feels in contact with nature:

> you ask me to run
> naked in the streets with you
> i am holding your pulse.

(4)

Much in the same spirit, Whitman writes in "Song of Myself":

> I will go to the bank by the wood and become undisguised and naked,
> I am mad for it to be in contact with me.

(*Complete Poetry* 25)

While immersing herself in nature, Sanchez from time to time subtly expresses her aversion to artificiality and domesticity. The first song in

"Naked in the Streets" begins with the lines "i cannot stay home / on this sweet morning / i must run singing laughing / through the streets of Philadelphia"(5). Invigorated by fresh air, inhaling the hot breath of her lover, she keeps singing her song. The urge Sanchez feels to cleanse herself of the unnatural and the artificial is reminiscent of Whitman's "Song of Myself":

> Houses and rooms are full of perfumes, the shelves are crowded with
>   perfumes,
> I breathe the fragrance myself and know it and like it,
> The distillation would intoxicate me also, but I shall not let it.
>
> (*Complete Poetry* 25)

Both Sanchez and classic Japanese haiku poets are always inspired by the visual beauty in which nature presents itself. Buson was well known in his time as a professional painter, just as he is today, and many of his haiku reflect his singular attention to color and its intensification. One of Sanchez's haiku included in the middle section, "Shake Loose My Skin," and one of the longer poems titled "A Poem for Ella Fitzgerald" both thrive on colorful imagery. Sanchez's haiku reads:

> i am you loving
> my own shadow watching
> this noontime butterfly.
>
> (61)

"A Poem for Ella Fitzgerald," the longest poem in this collection, is focused on such lines as "the moon turned red in the sky," "nightingales in her throat," "an apollo stage amid high-stepping / yellow legs," and "the sun downpoured yellow butterflies"(104–7). "Shake Loose My Skin" and "A Poem for Ella Fitzerald" are both reminiscent of Buson's "Also Stepping On," a haiku that can be compared to Wright's haiku "A butterfly makes / The sunshine even brighter / With fluttering wings," discussed in Chapter 7:

> Also stepping on
> The mountain pheasant's tail is
> The spring setting sun.[1]

For a seasonal reference to spring, Buson links an image of the bird with spring sunset, because both are highly colorful. As a painter he is also fascinated by an ambiguous impression the scene he has drawn gives him; it is not clear whether the setting sun is treading on the pheasant's tail or the tail on the setting sun. In any event, Buson has made both pictures beautiful to behold. In Sanchez's haiku, "I Am You Loving," it is ambivalent whether the focus is on "my own shadow" or "this noontime butterfly"; both constitute beautiful images of nature. Likewise "A Poem for Ella Fitzgerald" juxtaposes the image of the red moon with that of nightingales. Sanchez in these poems creates, as does Buson in his, a pair of counter images, themselves highly colorful and bright, which in turn intensify each other.

In portraying nature, Sanchez is at times puzzled by its spontaneous imagery. Two of the poems in the collection—"I Collect" (sonku) and "In This Wet Season" (haiku)—thrive on striking images and observations. "I Collect" begins with a query:

> i collect
> wings what are
> you bird or
> animal?

(15)

In the other poem

> in this wet season
> of children raining hands
> we catch birds in flight.

(103)

Sanchez is reluctant to draw a distinction between children and birds, hands and rain.

In emulating the spirit of nature, Japanese poets are often struck with awe and respect. American poets like Emerson, Dickinson, Pound, and Wright viewed nature from a similar vantage point, and Sanchez seems to have followed the same tradition. In keeping with this tradition, the haiku poet may not only aim at expressing sensation but also at generalizing and hence depersonalizing it. In a similar vein Sanchez expresses in "I Count the Morning" (8) and "I Come from the Same" (9), included in "Naked in the Streets," the pure sensation nature offers for human perception.

The predilection to portray human life in close association with nature means that the poet is more interested in genuinely natural sentiments than in moral, ethical, or political problems. Looking at the wind as a primal signifier of nature, Sanchez composed two poems in "Naked in the Streets," one titled "Haiku" and the other "Blues Haiku":

> Haiku
> how fast is the wind
> sailing? how fast did i go
> to become slow?
>
> (38)

> Blues Haiku
> let me be yo wil
> derness let me be yo wind
> blowing you all day.
>
> (39)

Traditionally, another singular, awe-inspiring signifier of nature in haiku is silence. Besides "The Old Pond," Basho is also known for another haiku that concerns nature's silence, "How Quiet It Is!" which was earlier compared to Wright's haiku on a similar subject:

> How quiet it is!
> Piercing into the rocks
> The cicada's voice.[2]

In the middle section of *Like the Singing Coming off the Drums*, "Shake Loose My Skin," Sanchez wrote this haiku:

> how still the morning sea
> how still this morning skin
> anointing the day.
>
> (50)

Just as Basho was awed by the silence pervading the backdrop of the scene in contrast to the shrilling cicada, Sanchez is struck by the equation between the stillness of "the morning sea" and that of "this morning skin." As pointed out earlier, Richard Wright, perhaps influenced by Basho, composed the following pair of haiku in which he focused on nature's silence:

In the silent forest
A woodpecker hammers at
The sound of silence.

(Wright, *Haiku* 79)

A thin waterfall
Dribbles the whole autumn night,—
How lonely it is.[3]

(Wright, *Haiku* 143)

What is common in these haiku by the three poets is that the scene is drawn with little detail, and the mood is provided by a simple, reserved description of fact. These haiku create the kind of beauty associated with the aesthetic sensibility of *sabi*, which suggests loneliness and quietude as opposed to overexcitement and loudness.[4]

Traditionally as well, the haiku in its portrayal of human beings' association with nature expresses the poet's enlightenment, a new way of looking at humanity and nature. In some of her poems in *Like the Singing Coming off the Drums*, Sanchez follows this tradition. The second stanza in "Love Poem [*for Tupac*]," "the old ones / say we don't / die we are / just passing / through into another space" (111), suggests Sanchez's fascination with the Buddhist theory of transmigration. The Buddhist concept of reincarnation has a striking affinity with the Akan concept of life and death in Wright's *Black Power*. Buddhism and the Akan religion share the belief, as does Lacan, that death is not the opposite of life but that death is a continuation of life.[5]

The following haiku expresses not only the concept of reincarnation, but also an enlightenment in Zen philosophy:

what is done is done
what is not done is not done
let it go . . . like the wind.

(27)

The last line "let it go . . . like the wind" spontaneously expresses the truth about nature and humanity. Some of Sanchez's haiku like this one have an affinity with the Zen concept of *mu*. This state of nothingness, as discussed earlier, is devoid of all thoughts and emotions that are derived from human subjectivity and egotism and contrary to the conscious or unconscious truth represented by nature. A person can be enlightened once he or she is liberated from the self-centered worldview, the convention, or the received opinion that lacks fairness and justice. While Sanchez, in the first two lines of this haiku, describes facts in human life, she in the last line gives an admonition as a Zen master that one must emulate the principles of nature in molding one's conduct and action.

Another haiku by Sanchez, included at the end of "Naked in the Streets," also concerns the Zen-like discipline of thought:

> let us be one with
> the earth expelling anger
> spirit unbroken.
>
> (44)

In the middle section of the book, titled "Shake Loose My Skin," Sanchez composed another Zen-inspired haiku:

> you are rock garden
> austere in your loving
> in exile from touch.
>
> (97)

In these haiku Sanchez tries to render the austerity of the human mind by viewing nature as a revelation.

Not only do many of Sanchez's haiku follow Zen doctrine, they also share the aesthetic principles that underlie classic haiku. One of the most delicate principles of Eastern art is called *yugen*, mentioned earlier. Originally *yugen* in Japanese art was an element of style pervasive in the language of *noh*. It was also a philosophical principle originated in Zen metaphysics. In Zen, every individual possesses Buddhahood and must realize it. *Yugen*, as applied to art, designates the mysterious and dark, whatever underlies the surface. The mode of expression, as noted earlier, is subtle as opposed to obvious, suggestive rather than declarative. *Yugen* functions in art as a means by which human beings can comprehend the course of nature. Although *yugen* seems allied with a sense of resignation, it has a far different effect on the human psyche. The style of *yugen* can express either happiness or sorrow.

The sense of loss also underlies the principle of *yugen*. Sanchez's first *tanka* "I Thought about You" in "Naked in the Street" expresses such a sentiment: "i thought about you / the pain of not having / you cruising my bones. / ... / ... / ..." (18). A pair of blues haiku, "When

We Say Good-bye" (16) and "You Too Slippery" (17), included in the same section, figure a brightened sense of *yugen* as well. As aesthetic principles, *yugen* and the blues share the sentiments derived from private and personal feelings. As modes of expression, the blues stylistically differs from *yugen* since, as Amiri Baraka has observed, the blues "issued directly out of the shout and of course the spiritual" (62). Whereas *yugen* is characterized by reservation and modesty, the blues tradition calls for a worldly excitement and love. Unlike *yugen*, the blues confines its attention solely to the immediate and celebrates the bodily expression: both "When We Say Good-bye" and "You Too Slippery" convey direct, unreserved sexual manifestations. Most importantly, Sanchez tries to link the blues message with sexually charged language so as to liberate black bodies from the distorted images slavery inflicted.

That the blues tradition has a greater impact on Sanchez's poetry than does the aesthetics of *yugen* can be seen in the way Sanchez constructs her imagery. If imagery in classic haiku is regarded as indirect and suggestive, the imagery in Sanchez's poetry has the directness and clarity of good prose, as opposed to the suggestiveness and vagueness of symbolist poetry. The first poem in "Naked in the Streets" has an extremely sensuous image: dancing is described in terms of "corpuscles sliding in blood" (3). In the second poem of the same section, a haiku quoted earlier, the central image of running "naked in the streets" does not suggest anything other than what it describes:

> you ask me to run
> naked in the streets with you
> i am holding your pulse.

(4)

Such a poem as "You Ask Me to Run" bears a structural resemblance to Pound's famous imagistic haiku, "In a Station of the Metro," quoted earlier. Unlike Sanchez's haiku, Pound's "In a Station of the Metro" is constructed in two lines simply because Pound had in mind "a form of super-position" in which the poem was to be composed. "In a poem of this sort," he explained, "one is trying to record the precise instant when a thing outward and objective transforms itself, or darts into a thing inward and subjective" ("Vorticism" 467). Compared to Pound's "In a Station of the Metro," Sanchez's "You Ask Me to Run" has a similar structure in imagery. Just as in "Legs Wrapped Around You," Sanchez in "You Ask Me to Run" is trying to record the precise instant when a thing outward and objective, that is, running "naked in the streets," transforms itself or darts into a thing inward and subjective, that is, the image of "i am holding your pulse." The image of running naked in the streets is based in immediate experience, whether real or imagined, since Sanchez lived in Philadelphia. Not only did she see the "thing," it must have generated such a sensation that she could not shake it out of her mind.

Most discussions about the genesis of the Imagist movement are speculative at best. Pound's insistence that an image in poetry must be active rather than passive suggests that a modernist poem like Pound's and Sanchez's is not a description of something, but, as Aristotle had said of tragedy, an action. Pound approaches Aristotelianism in his insistence that the image of the faces in the crowd in his metro poem was not simply a description of his sensation at the station, but an active entity capable of dynamic development. According to his experience, this particular image instantly transformed itself into another image, the image of the petals on a wet, black bough. To Pound, the success of this poem resulted from his instantaneous perception of the relatedness between the two entirely different objects. Although in Sanchez's poems the two related objects are not entirely different, as in Pound's "In a Station of the Metro," Sanchez's images are strikingly active and instantaneous rather than symbolic and suggestive.

2

Although most of the short poems collected in *Like the Singing Coming off the Drums* are stylistically influenced by the poetics of haiku as well as by the aesthetics of modernist poetry, much of Sanchez's ideological concern is postmodern, postcolonial, and African American. Many of her poems aim at teaching African Americans to achieve individualism and value their heritage. Even such a haiku as

> mixed with day and sun
> i crouched in the earth carry
> you like a dark river.

(36)

succinctly expresses what Langston Hughes does in "The Negro Speaks of Rivers." Hughes reminds readers of the ancient rivers such as the Euphrates, the Congo, and the Nile, and then leads them to the most important river for African Americans, the Mississippi. Hughes evokes

Abraham Lincoln, who "went down to New Orleans, and I've seen its muddy bosom turn all golden in the sunset" (*Selected Poems* 4). Sanchez and Hughes are both portraying how the African American soul, a symbol of humanity, is deeply embedded in the earth. The soul, as Hughes sees, "has grown deep like the rivers"; anyone endowed with it, like Sanchez, carries anyone else "like a dark river."

Hughes's signifying thrives on a chain of signs, signifiers, and signifieds. While "the Euphrates," "the Congo," "the Nile," and "the Mississippi" are all great rivers, they also signify different human histories. All the signifieds in turn signify yet other historical events. For African Americans, "the Mississippi" signifies its "singing . . . when Abe Lincoln went down to New Orleans"; not only does it signify "its muddy bosom," but its signified in turn signifies a beautiful image, the golden river under sunset. Sanchez's haiku, on the other hand, is comprised of fewer but nonetheless equally powerful signs, signifiers, and signifieds: the words *mixed, day, sun, i, crouched, earth, carry, you, dark,* and *river.* These words express natural, spontaneous human sentiments, as do those in classic haiku, rather than emotional, personal feelings. In fact, an epiphany given in Sanchez's haiku, "Mixed with Day and Sun," bears a strong resemblance to a cross-cultural vision captured in Hughes's "The Negro Speaks of Rivers."

Sanchez's most important thematic concern is love of humanity, an act of faith that must begin with self-love. The last poem in the collection, dedicated to Gwendolyn Brooks, is a response and rejoinder to such a poem as Brooks's "The Mother." Not only is Brooks portrayed as "a holy one," but also she has become a universal symbol of the mother with enduring love and humanity. Sanchez's apotheosis of Gwendolyn Brooks ends with the lines "breathe and love and / breath her . . . /this Gwensister called life" (133). The sign that Sanchez's "For Sister Gwen Brooks" shares with Brooks's "The Mother" signifies the universal vision that love emanates from a mother. Sanchez's refrain "for she is a holy one" further signifies the goddess worshiped among the Ashanti and the female king who owns her children, as described in Richard Wright's *Black Power.* In *Pagan Spain*, as Wright speculates, the universal motherhood has derived from the Virgin Mary, "Maya, the mother of Buddha," and "Isis, mother of Horus." As Wright remarks, "Egyptians worshiped Isis . . . and she was called Our Lady, the Queen of Heaven, Mother of God" (*Pagan Spain* 65).

In "The Mother," Brooks, referring to the issue of abortion as a sign, makes it signify the universal issue of love. The opening lines graphically describe the lifeless fetuses:

Abortions will not let you forget.
You remember the children you got that you did not get,
The damp small pulps with a little or with no hair,

"The damp small pulps," a signified, in turn signifies "[the] singers and workers," the objects of motherly love, who would have flourished if their unborn bodies had not been aborted: "You will never wind up the sucking-thumb / Or scuttle off ghosts that come." Brooks as a mother expresses her remorse for aborting her children as if she committed a crime: "If I stole your births and your names, / Your straight baby tears and your games, / Your stilted or lovely loves, your tumults, your marriages, / aches, and your deaths."

Toward the end of the poem, however, the issue of abortion signifies that of nurture. Millions of children the world over, born of poverty and neglect, are Brooks's ultimate issue and concern. While the poem, on the surface, depicts the abortion of fetuses, Brooks appeals to the moral conscience of adults with profound love and compassion for children. The poem is also a social protest in allusion to the issue of nurturing children instead of a debate on the issue of abortion in itself. Brooks is not arguing against abortion per se; she is indicting society of undernourishing and undereducating the children of the poor. "You were born," she stresses, "you had body, you died / It is just that you never giggled or planned or cried" (*Selected Poems* 4–5). Brooks agonizes over the callousness of society, which stunted and killed children, who would have become "singers and workers." "The Mother," then, reads as an admonition that neglect of children is the fault of society, not that of the mother. It is only natural and universal that a mother should love a child; it is unnatural and immoral that society should refuse to nurture children.

The penultimate poem in *Like the Singing Coming off the Drums* is dedicated to Cornel West. In contrast to the rest of the poems, it is a prose poem like Whitman's "Song of Myself." Cornel West, a Harvard professor, is not presented as a spokesman of the academia but characterized as a cultural activist like Whitman, Hughes, and Brooks, each of whom in a unique way sought to apotheosize the humanity of the land. Sanchez sees West as a foremost individual at the dawn of the twenty-first century, a spokesperson always "questioning a country that denies the sanctity, the holiness of children, people, rivers, sky, trees, earth" (130). Sanchez urges the reader to "look at the father in him. The husband in him. The activist in him. The teacher in him. The lover in him. The truth seeker in him. The James Brown dancer in him. The reformer in him. The defender of people in him. The intellectual in him" (130–31). West is, Sanchez continues, "This man. Born into history. This humanist. This twenty-first-century traveler pulling us screaming against our will towards a future that will hold all of humankind in an embrace. He acknowledges us all. The poor. Blacks and whites. Asians and Native Americans. Jews and Muslims. Latinos and Africans. Gays and Lesbians" (131).[6] Rather than dwelling on the racial conflict and oppression the country has suffered, Sanchez admonishes the reader to see cross-pollination in the various cultures brought together to the land.

Whether *Like the Singing Coming off the Drums* is Sanchez's best work remains to be seen in the generations to come, but an effort to use diverse principles of aesthetics in molding her poetry has few precedents in American literature. Thematically, nineteenth-century American writers like Emerson, Poe, Dickinson, and Whitman were partly influenced by various cultural and religious thoughts, just as twentieth-century American writers like Ezra Pound, Wallace Stevens, Richard Wright, Allen Ginsberg, Jack Kerouac, and Gary Snyder at some points in their careers emulated Eastern poetics. Sanchez, on the other hand, remains one of the accomplished contemporary American poets writing from the perspective of cross-cultural visions for the form and content of her poetry.

CHAPTER 9

JAMES EMANUEL'S JAZZ HAIKU

While haiku is a traditional Japanese poetic form, jazz has its origin in African American music. Despite technical differences in composition, haiku and jazz have been known for the powerful expressions of human sentiments by celebrated artists in both genres. *Jazz from the Haiku King* (1999) is the latest collection of Emanuel's work, in which a contemporary African American poet has presented a series of literary experiments he calls "jazz haiku."[1] As jazz has crossed cultural boundaries the world over in modern times, Emanuel's intention is to translate the musical expressions of African American life, its pain and joy, into the 5-7-5 syllabic measures of haiku. In so doing, he has also attempted to expand the imagery of the traditional haiku beyond its single impression by including narrative and rhyme.

In Japanese culture, haiku, as noted earlier, has served as an expression of the unity and harmony of all things, a sensibility that humanity and nature are one and inseparable. By the 1680s, haiku with its master, Basho, had become a highly stylized expression of poetic vision.[2] Not only was Basho the founder of the poetic genre, but he also had many distinguished disciples, such as Ransetsu and Kikaku. Basho also paved the way for the celebrated haiku poets in later periods, such as Buson and Issa. Then in the late 1950s, two American novelists, Jack Kerouac and Richard Wright, tried their hand at writing haiku and succeeded in their endeavor. Sonia Sanchez and James A. Emanuel, while influenced by Wright, who had been influenced by classic Japanese haiku poets like Basho, Buson, and Issa, have in turn incorporated the African American musical tradition centering on jazz and the blues into the Japanese poetic tradition.

Even on the surface there is much in common between jazz and haiku. As jazz performance thrives on an endless improvisation that the composer makes out of traditional materials, so does haiku composition on an infinite improvisation on beautiful objects in nature and humanity. Because of improvisation, the composer in both genres must efface his or her identity. In jazz, play changes on ideas as well as on sounds, thus creating unexpected sensations. In haiku, the poet spares no pains to capture unexpected sensations. In both genres, the composer and the composed, subject and object, coalesce as the identity of the composer disappears in the wake of creation.

Jazz also shares many of the philosophical principles that underlie haiku. Since Basho's time, haiku has traditionally been associated with Zen philosophy. Zen teaches the follower to attain enlightenment, a new way of looking at humanity and nature. Just as Zen stresses self-reliance, not egotism, and nature, not materialism, so does jazz. Like haiku, jazz, characterized by innovation, seeks a new way of looking at ourselves and the world around us. As jazz challenges us to hear the sounds and rhythms we have not heard before, so does haiku to see the images of humanity and nature we have not seen before. Jazz and haiku enable us to open our minds and imagine ways of reaching a higher ground in our present lives.

1

Unlike the origin and development of haiku, those of jazz are well known by African American writers. Although jazz originated in the South from the blues and spirituals, it evolved into city music, flourishing with the Harlem Renaissance in the 1920s and with the Chicago Renaissance in the late 1930s and the early 1940s. As African Americans migrated to the northern cities, they bore with them what Ralph Ellison called "the painful details and episodes of a brutal experience alive in one's aching consciousness, to finger its jagged grain, and to transcend it, not by the consolation of philosophy but by squeezing from it a near-tragic, near comic lyricism" ("Wright's Blues" 202).[3] To Richard Wright, the jazz or the spirituals convey "bitter rebellion" that "simmers" behind them. When hearing such music, Wright stressed, one must not erase the fact that hatred is what constitutes African American life, "the hatred of the disinherited from which no black man can isolate himself" (*Conversations* 108).

Not only did Wright and Ellison agree that African American music is a poignant expression of painful experience, but they also observed that it is a most effective means by which to battle against racism.

African American music, as a cultural critique, deconstructs the power of authority. Music decenters the outdated authority and creates in its place a new authority, what Alan Nadel calls "one composed of subversive strategies drawing from African-American traditions of 'call & response,' 'signifyin',' and 'loud talking'" (Werner, *Playing* xix).

As African music, the blues has served as an artistic and metaphoric ideal of freedom and individualism. Langston Hughes, a central figure of the Harlem Renaissance in the 1920s, wrote a series of poems collected in *The Weary Blues* (1926), celebrating the African American experience and inspiring African Americans to achieve individualism and self-reliance despite their adversity and loneliness. In "The Weary Blues" he provides a portrayal of a blues singer: Hughes makes the blues singer say, "Ain't got nobody in all this world, / Ain't got nobody but ma self" (*Selected Poems* 33). Despite adversity and racism, the blues singer's life thrives on courage, independence, and individualism. To Hughes, the blues was a response to an unjust, unnatural racist system of power that had consistently degraded and denied African American experience.

Unlike Hughes, Wright believed that the blues represents a simplistic form of African American vernacular aesthetics. In his foreword to Paul Oliver's *Blues Fell This Morning*, Wright characterizes the blues with "a vocabulary terser than Basic English, shorn of all hyperbole, purged of metaphysical implications, wedded to a frankly atheistic vision of life, and excluding almost all references to *nature* and her various moods" (viii, emphasis added). In *12 Million Black Voices*, Wright describes the blues as a passive form of musical expression: "The ridiculousness and sublimity of love are captured in our blues, those sad-happy songs that laugh and weep all in one breath, those mockingly tender utterances of a folk imprisoned in steel and stone" (128).

At the opening scene in *Native Son*, Bigger's mother sings,

> *Life is like a mountain railroad*
> *With an engineer that's brave*
> *We must make the run successful*
> *From the cradle to the grave . . .*

(*Native Son* 14)

"The song," Wright remarks, "irked him and he was glad when she stopped and came into the room with a pot of coffee and a plate of crinkled bacon" (14). Later in the story, Jan argues that a Communist revolution needs African Americans, who have "spirit," and says, "And their songs—the spirituals! Aren't they marvelous?" Bigger says he can't sing but Mary Dalton, closing her eyes, sings,

> "Swing low, sweet chariot,
> Coming fer to carry me home. . . ."

Although Jan joins in, Bigger, Wright comments, "smiled derisively. Hell, that ain't the tune, he thought" (76–77).

As the migration from the South to Chicago and other Great Lakes cities continued in the early decades of the twentieth century, the sacred traditions of the Southern black church developed into the gospel music of Clara Ward, Roberta Martin, and Mahalia Jackson. This gospel music "in turn contributed to the vocal styles fundamental to fifties rhythm and blues and sixties soul music" (Werner, *Playing* 244). Along with the musical developments, Wright organized a series of meetings for African American writers and artists, establishing the South Side Writers' Group in 1936. In such meetings he submitted for discussions his essays and his drafts of "Down by the Riverside," "Long Black Song," and "Bright and Morning Star" (Fabre, *Unfinished Quest* 128).

In contrast to the blues and the spirituals, jazz is well known for improvisation and syncopation. In addition to individualism, which also distinguishes jazz, another salient feature of jazz is the anonymity of jazz artists, as Ellison observes:

> Some of the most brilliant of jazzmen made no records; their names appeared in print only in announcements of some local dance or remote "battles of music" against equally uncelebrated bands. Being devoted to an art which traditionally thrives on improvisation, these unrecorded artists very often have their most original ideas enter the public domain almost as rapidly as they are conceived to be quickly absorbed into the thought and technique of their fellows. Thus the riffs which swung the dancers and the band on some transcendent evening, and which inspired others to competitive flights of invention, become all too swiftly a part of the general style, leaving the originator as anonymous as the creators of the architecture called Gothic. (*Shadow* 234)

The anonymity of jazz musicians has an affinity with that of *noh* dramatists. W. B. Yeats, inspired by *noh* drama, wrote such plays as *At the Hawk's Well*. In the performance of the play, discussed in Chapter 4, Yeats used masks to present anonymous, time-honored expressions, just as the Roman theater used masks instead of makeup (Noguchi, *Spirit of Japanese Poetry* 60). Yeats clearly implied in his letter to Yone Noguchi that contemporary arts in the West were infected with egotism, while classical works of art in Japan were created as if anonymously (Noguchi, *Selected Writings* 2: 14).

What seemed to have inspired Yeats was the "simplicity" of the artists, an ancient form of beauty that transcends time, place, and personality. Irked by modern ingenuity and science, he was adamantly opposed to realism in art and literature. For him, realism failed to uncover the deeply ingrained human spirit and character. He later discovered that noble spirits and profound emotions are expressed with simplicity in the *noh* play. Noguchi observed, "It was the time when nobody asked who wrote them, if the plays themselves were worthy. What a difference from this day of advertisement and personal ambition! . . . I mean that they are not the creation of one time or one age; it is not far wrong to say that they wrote themselves, as if flowers or trees rising from the rich soil of tradition and Buddhistic faith" (*Spirit of Japanese Poetry* 63). In its simplicity and appeal, jazz has much in common with *noh* drama.

Unlike the blues, jazz is characterized by its flexibility and creativity. As the blues emphasizes individuality and personality, jazz does anonymity and impersonality. While both individuality and communal affirmation are central to the blues, their relationship and importance to jazz are different from those to the blues. "Seen in relation to the blues impulse," Craig Werner observes, "the jazz impulse provides a way of exploring implications of realizing the relational possibilities of the (blues) self, and of expanding the consciousness of self and community through a process of continual improvisation" (*Playing* xxii). Involving both self-expression and community affirmation, jazz is a genre of ambivalence and of what Ellison calls "a cruel contradiction." He remarks, "For true jazz is an art of individual assertion within and against the group. Each true jazz moment (as distinct from the uninspired commercial performance) springs from a contest in which each artist challenges all the rest; each solo flight, or improvisation, represents (like the successive canvasses of a painter) a definition of his identity: as individual, as member of the collectivity and as a link in the chain of tradition" (*Shadow* 234). In light of the relation of self and community, jazz also bears a strong resemblance to *renga*, the Japanese linked song, from which haiku evolved. *Renga*, which flourished in the beginning as comic poetry, was a continuous chain of fourteen (7-7) and seventeen (5-7-5) syllable verses, each independently composed but connected as one poem, a communal composition.[4]

In practice, however, jazz in the early 1950s emphasized individuality, in technical virtuosity and theoretical knowledge, rather than community and its involvement with jazz. "In response," Werner notes, "jazz musicians such as Miles Davis, Ornett Coleman, and John Coltrane established the contours of the multifaceted 'free jazz' movement, which includes most AACM [the Association for the Advancement of Creative Musicians] work" (*Playing* 247). As Gayl Jones has also remarked, jazz, rendered through nonchronological syncopation and tempo, thrives on the essence of jazz, "the jam session," that "emerges from an interplay of voices improvising on the basic themes or motifs of the text in keywords and phrases." This interplay of self and other and self and community, what Jones calls "seemingly nonlogical and associational," makes the jazz text more complex, flexible, and fluid than the blues text (*Liberating* 200). Jazz, as Louis Armstrong said, is a genre of music that should never be played in the same way as before.[5]

While jazz has served African Americans as an artistic medium for conveying pain and suffering, it has also expressed natural human desire. Toni Morrison's *Jazz*, as I have maintained elsewhere, is intended not only as a battle against racism but also, more importantly, as a blueprint for fulfillment of desire by African Americans. The novel demonstrates that only when "the village within" is established in the city will they be able to fulfill their desire. Morrison's attempt to equate desire with sexuality through jazz is corroborated by Wright's view of jazz. Wright was familiarly known as "Dick" in Harlem. He told Frank Tenot, an interviewer, "The black bourgeoisie don't like either [gospel or jazz], because in their anxiety to imitate whites, they consider both to be 'primitive' art forms, incapable of expressing lofty, 'civilized' sentiments." Wright believed that the African American bourgeoisie's taste for music was corrupted by Hollywood music and American musicals, the type of music he called "Very bad music." In sum, he told Tenot, "Not to be a black bourgeois and to understand that the main gift that jazz has to offer the world today is an affirmation of *desire*" (*Conversations* 242–43).

Wright's emphasis on the aspect of jazz as an expression of desire notwithstanding, jazz has a strong affinity with haiku. Not only are jazz and haiku well-established art forms, they are both in sharp antithesis to materialism and commercialism. Little wonder Wright regarded Hollywood music and American musicals as vulgar representations of materialism and capitalism, to which he was averse all his life. The four thousand haiku he wrote in his final eighteen months poignantly express his conviction that materialism and its corollary, greed, were the twin culprits of racial conflict.

Jazz is also a catalyst for African Americans to attain their individualism. Ellison and Wright clearly differ in achieving African American individualism. Ellison defines jazz as a means of expressing individualism in relation to collectivity and tradition. Wright, on the other hand, defines writing as a means of expressing individuality independent of collectivity and tradition. In "Blueprint for Negro Writing," Wright envisions African American individualism as buttressed by the twin pillars of "perspective" and "intellectual space" that must not be influenced by any traditions or world movements. "At its best," he stresses, "perspective is a pre-conscious assumption, something which a writer takes for granted, something which he wins through his living" (45–46). The reason for his defection from the Communist Party was that Communists deprived him of his individuality. In defining African American narrative of "ascent" and "immersion," Robert Stepto shows that ascent narrative, diverting from familial or communal postures, develops into "a new posture in the least oppressive environment—at best one of solitude; at worst, one of alienation" (*Veil* 167).

In *Jazz*, African American individualism finds its expressions and representations in the various events that Toni Morrison explores in the novel. At first she focuses on the courtship of Violet and Joe. For them, individualism does not simply mean freedom from racial oppression in American life; it is a sign of creation and progression, the twin actions the urban mood and music is urging on them. Paradoxically, lack of space in the city creates more action and generates more desire: "Her hip bones rubbed his thigh as they stood in the aisle unable to stop smiling." The rhythm of jazz represents an undulating movement that urges the listener into individuality rather than conformity. Just as Hollywood music and American musicals conform to materialistic and commercial impulses, African American jazz, in its freely improvised and syncopated sounds and rhythms, expresses subjective and individualistic sentiments. "However they came, when or why," Morrison writes in *Jazz*, "the minute the leather of their soles hit the pavement—there was no turning around" (32). Likewise, the sound of drums has the effect of urging on a mature, middle-aged African American woman like Alice Manfred to seek liberty and happiness, but more importantly it inspires her with a sense of individuality and responsibility.

2

As many of the modern African American writers have been inspired by jazz, so is James Emanuel. His poetry, moreover, as the title of the book indicates, seeks a means of expression shared by jazz and haiku. Jazz and haiku both convey spontaneously created expressions that are free from any economic, social, or political impulses. "Jazz," he writes in his preface, "I knew—like the Caruso I heard on the same phonograph—had no boundaries; but its immense international magnetism seemed inadequately explored in poetry" (iv–v). In haiku, despite its brevity, he found much of the height and depth of vision as he did in jazz.

In the haiku "Dizzy's Bellows Pumps," under the title "Dizzy Gillespie (News of His Death,)" placed in the middle of the collection,

> Dizzy's bellows pumps.
> Jazz balloon inflates, floats high.
> Earth listens, stands by.

(44)

Emanuel hears Gillespie's music reverberate in the sky and on earth. Traditionally, haiku express and celebrate the unity of humanity and nature: a part of a haiku usually has a *kigo* (seasonal word). Even though Emanuel's "Dizzy's Bellows Pumps" lacks a seasonal reference, it displays the nexus of humanity and nature: Gillespie and sky and earth. This haiku is an elegy as Whitman's "When Lilacs Last in the Dooryard Bloom'd" is an elegy for Lincoln. In celebrating the lives of great men, both poems express the immortality of their spirits. As Lincoln will return with lilacs in the spring and the northern star at night, Gillespie will be remembered for his jazz.

Emanuel's haiku on Gillespie is also remindful of Zen philosophy, which emphasizes the fusion of humanity and nature. Zen teaches its followers to transcend the dualism of life and death. Zen master Dogen observed that life and death are not as separate as they seem and that there is no need to avoid death. Similarly, Emanuel and Whitman both seek a reconciliation of life and death. Whitman's feat of turning the national bereavement in the elegy into a celebration of death is well known, but less known is his idea of death given in "A Sight in Camp in the Daybreak Gray and Dim." To Whitman, the dead soldier in this poem appears no less divine than the savior Christ; they both represent the living Godhead. In a similar vein, as

Gillespie's jazz balloon floats high in the sky and the earth stands by and listens, this jazz master is vividly alive.

Emanuel captures the affinity of jazz and haiku in many of the poems in the collection. The first chapter, "Page One," features various types of jazz haiku with translations into other languages: "The Haiku King," "Jazzanatomy," "Jazzroads," "Jazzactions," and "Bojangles and Jo." The first of the four poems under the group title "Jazzanatomy" reads,

> EVERYTHING is jazz:
> snails, jails, rails, tails, males, females,
> snow-white   cotton bales.

> (2)

To Emanuel, jazz represents all walks of life, human and nonhuman alike. Human life is represented by males and females, animal life by snails and tails, and inanimate life by snow-white. "My haiku," Emanuel remarks in his preface, "added the toughness of poverty and racial injustice" (iv). The images of "jails" and "cotton bales," signifying the unjustified imprisonment of African Americans and their immoral slave labor, represent the twin evils in American life: racism and poverty. "Song of Myself," a narrative and autobiographical poem by Whitman, also concerns all walks of American life. Focusing on human life, Whitman declares, "I am the poet of the Body and I am the poet of the Soul," and "I am the poet of the woman the same as the man." About the problems of good and evil, he writes, "The pleasures of heaven are with me and the pains of hell are with me" (*Complete Poetry* 39).

Emanuel's view of humanity and nature is shared by his American predecessors, such as Whitman, Countee Cullen, and Wright. The opening pages of Wright's *Black Power* has a passage addressed "To the Unknown African" and two quotations from Cullen and Whitman. "To the Unknown African" records an observation derived from Wright's view that the African was victimized by slave trades because of the African's primal outlook on human existence. The quotations from both Cullen and Whitman suggest that Africans, the inheritors and products of nature, have been exploited by a materialistic civilization. Before Europeans appeared with their machines, the continent had thrived on its pastoral idylls. Now it exists at the services of Western traders who exploit African products. Whitman's line "*Not till the sun excludes you do I exclude you,*" quoted in *Black Power*, expresses not merely his compassion for African Americans but strongly, as do Cullen's lines, their natural and divine heritage.[6]

Emanuel's attempt to unify human and natural spirits can be seen in many of his jazz haiku. What underlies his experimentation is a Jeffersonian belief that those who live and work intimately with the earth deserve divine protection.[7] In the haiku "Good-grip Jazz, Farmer," Emanuel depicts the affinity of a farmer with jazz:

> Good-grip Jazz, farmer:
> ploughed music like fields, worked late,
> kept all furrows straight.

> (64)

Inspirational jazz is like a God-chosen farmer who cultivates the earth to attain the spirit of nature. The earth, to Thomas Jefferson, is "the focus in which he [God] keeps alive that sacred fire, which otherwise might escape from the face of the earth" (Jefferson 165). To Emanuel, jazz inspires genuine spirits as the farmer keeps "all furrows straight." The word *straight* has a moral implication if this haiku is remindful of Jefferson's notes on farmers. "Corruption of morals in the mass of cultivators," Jefferson maintains, "is a phænomenon of which no age nor nation has furnished an example" (Jefferson 165). Unlike the traditional haiku with a single image or a juxtaposition of two separate images, Emanuel's "Farmer" portrays a pair of related actions in farming. Not only does a good farmer, like a good jazz musician, work "late," but he also keeps "all furrows straight."

The confluence of haiku and jazz in Emanuel's poems is based on the expression of natural, spontaneous responses to human life. This sensibility is distinguished from that of negotiation and ambivalence characteristic of social and political discourse. The first group of poems, "Jazzanatomy," presents, besides "EVERYTHING Is Jazz," three other jazz haiku. The first haiku features the explosive sound produced by a percussion instrument: "Knee-bone, thigh, hip-bone. / Jazz slips you percussion boneclassified 'unknown'"(2). The last two, "Sleek Lizard Rhythms" and "Second-Chance Rhythms," (2) focus on the uniqueness of jazz rhythms. "Sleek Lizard Rhythms" characterizes the jazz rhythms as not only smooth like lizards but capable of making thin tunes rise high as "straight-gin sky." In the other one, "Second-Chance Rhythms," Emanuel hears the rhythms getting "HIGH" by not giving up riffs. The height such rhythms attain enables the composer to rise above "can'ts, buts, and ifs."

Emanuel's jazz haiku, "Second-Chance Rhythms," bears a resemblance to Basho's "The Old Pond." Emanuel describes the ways in which the sound of jazz, transcending social and political interests and conflicts, attains his peace of mind, just as Basho intimates his enlightenment by hearing the sound of the water bursting out of the tranquility of the world.

Emanuel's "Second-Chance Rhythms" is also reminiscent of Emily Dickinson's poem "The Soul Selects Her Own Society" in its rhythm. Emanuel suggests the attitude of flexibility by describing jazz rhythms as having riffs, two or four or more refrains, in them. But he also stresses the decisiveness of jazz by capitalizing the word "HIGH." In Dickinson's poem, the flexibility in a woman's character is described by longer lines with four beats, such as the opening line of each stanza:

> The Soul selects her own Society—
> . . . .
> Unmoved—she notes the Chariots—pausing—
> . . . .
> I've known her—from an ample nation—

By contrast, the decisiveness in the woman's character is expressed by shorter staccato lines with two beats, such as the concluding line of each stanza:

> Present no more—
> . . . .
> Upon her Mat—
> . . . .
> Like Stone—

> (*Complete Poems* 143)

Traditional haiku, seeking enlightenment on the spirit of nature, depicts the setting sun and the moon, mountains and seas, flowers and trees, and the like, but it does not concern human sexuality. Some contemporary haiku in America and Japan, however, are natural, spontaneous expressions of sexual desire, just as some forms of jazz are conducive to expressing sexuality. Rich Youmans, a contemporary American haiku poet, for example, includes such a haiku in his *haibun* (haiku essay) entitled "For My Wife on Our First Anniversary." Youmans describes scenes of nature in early spring, when he wakes at dawn and gazes at his sleeping wife. Such a passage, with its Christian allusions, makes this *haibun* an aubade, a kind of morning love lyric.

What this haiku poet experiences is an epiphany from the spirit of nature, the essential meaning of his life, his wife being both eros and agape. Her waking voice is related to an allusion to the Resurrection dogwood petals described as "cruciform." Youmans evokes the spirit of nature by the morning light transformed into prisms through the window glass, a figurative spiritualization of the physical world. The *haibun* ends with this haiku:

> prisms in
> early light:
> we make love

(Youmans 15)

Just as Youmans seeks enlightenment on sexual love through a Christian revelation, so does Emanuel through jazz music. The first chapter, "Page One," ends with four jazz haiku under the title "Bojangles and Jo." In Emanuel's jazz haiku "Stairstep Music: Ups" and "She Raised Champagne Lips," the jazz music with "ups" and "downs" induces Bill Robinson to smile and jazz-dance "the rounds." His smiling and jazz-dancing, in turn, leads to Josephine's raising "champagne lips" and dancing "inside banana hips": "All Paris" woos her. In the next pair of jazz haiku (80), "banana panties," "perfumed belt," and "JAZZ tattooing" each throw his listeners into "lush ecstasies." All in all, this jazz music makes her "royal": she reigns as a goddess of love, "the bosom of France." Not only does Emanuel cast "Bojangles and Jo" in a narrative style, but this group of jazz haiku also bears some resemblance to *renga*, Japanese linked song in the haiku manner.[8]

Emanuel's other unlinked, independently composed haiku are also jazzlike expressions of robust, natural human sexuality. His jazz haiku "Duke Ellington" begins with the first line "I love you madly," as his other jazz haiku "Fashion Show" incites his audience with the first line "When you rock those hips" (32). In "Duke Ellington," their "jazz hammock," endlessly rocking, inspires them with love. In "Fashion Show," rocking "those hips" and turning "like that" instantly generate male desire.

Another group of haiku, entitled "'I'm a Jazz Singer,' She Replied," is headed by an introductory haiku, "He Dug What She Said":

> He dug what she said:
> bright jellies, smooth marmalade
> spread on warm brown bread.

(83)

Each of the four other haiku in the group begins with the word "Jazz": "'Jazz' from drowsy lips," "'Jazz': quick fingerpops," and "'Jazz': cool banister" (83). In contrast to the linked haiku in "Bojangles and Jo," each of the haiku in "'I'm a Jazz Singer,' She Replied" is independently composed. Whereas those linked haiku capture the interactions between the jazz musicians in depicting the generation of sexual desire, each of these haiku about a certain female jazz singer features a specific image characteristic of the singer: "drowsy lips," "long sips," "quick fingerpops," and "mysterious / . . . missing fingers." Focusing on such sensuous images and actions, each of the haiku inspires the audience to generate desire and love.

3

From a philosophical perspective, Emanuel's jazz haiku has an affinity with the Zen concept of *mu*. A series of ten haiku in the chapter "Jazz Meets the Abstract (Engravings)," for example, describe various human actions in which Emanuel is in search of space, a Zen-like state of nothingness. This space is devoid of egotism and artificiality: it transcends human reasoning and personal vision. In the first haiku,

> Space moves, contours grow
> as wood, web, damp, dust. Points turn,
> Corners follow. JAZZ!

> (87)

Jazz creates a space that moves as its contours "grow / as wood, web, damp, dust," their points "turn," and their corners "follow." Neither intellectuality nor an emotion such as hatred and anger is able to occupy such a space.

Emanuel further shows, in his jazz haiku, the state of nothingness, which jazz is able to achieve:

> No meaning at birth:
> just screams, squirms, frowns without sight,
> fists clenched against light.

> (88)

Jazz is like a newborn child with its "fists clenched against light." The child just "screams, squirms, frowns without sight": all this has "No meaning at birth," a state of nothingness. In the next pair of jazz haiku,

"Abstract, I Try You" (90) and "No Dust, Rust, No Guilt" (93), Emanuel tries jazz, as he does an infant, "(walk, sit, stretch)." Like the infant, jazz says "nothing," *mu*, but is a good fit. Such a space has "No dust, rust," and such a state of mind has "no guilt." Whereas jazz was born and reared in America, it has attracted "guests from ALL lands." To Emanuel, jazz and Zen, characteristic of their respective cultures, have a common, universal appeal.

In other jazz haiku, he also envisions the world in which the state of *mu* can be attained. In this haiku, for example,

> Soars, leapfrogs, yells: JAZZ!
> But don't expect no tantrums,
> no crazyman spells.

(6)

height and intensity define jazz: it "Soars, leapfrogs, yells." Emanuel cautions, however, that soaring sounds and "yells" do not signal "tantrums" and "crazyman spells." The sound of jazz, like the sound of the water made by a leaping frog in Basho's haiku, signifies enlightenment, the state of *mu*. Just as Basho is impressed with the depth and silence of the universe, so is Emanuel with the height and intensity of jazz. This state of consciousness that jazz creates has the effect of cleansing the human mind of impurity. The haiku on Louis Armstrong,

> Jazz-rainbow: skywash
> his trumpet blew, cleansing air,
> his wonderworld there.

(56)

captures Armstrong's ability to create his utopia, a "wonderworld," purified of social ills and racial conflicts.

Armstrong's utopia is, in turn, buttressed by individualism. The last four haiku under the title "Steppin' Out on the Promise" in Chapter 5, "Jazzmix," urge on African Americans the imperative of individualism. The first pair of jazz haiku, "Step out, Brother. Blow" and "Step out, Sister. Blow" (84), address Brother and Sister, respectively. Emanuel impels each of the African American brothers and sisters to be individualistic, self-reliant in their efforts to realize the Promised Land. He tells his brother to blow his horn and plant "gold seeds" from it; he tells his sister to blow her horn and play the way God told her. The second pair, "Step out, Daughter. Shine" and "Step out, Sonny. Blow" (84), then, address Daughter and Sonny. Emanuel urges his daughter to shine in her performance and make her audience "jazzophile," just as he tells his son to blow his horn and enlighten his audience with "all they need to know." Emanuel's command "Step out," which begins each of the jazz haiku, emphasizes the principles of subjectivity and individuality in jazz performance. Each of the jazz haiku above, unlike a classic haiku, is united in its rhythm and meaning by a rhyme between the last two lines: "corn" and "horn," "play" and "way," "chile" and "jazzophile," "know" and "GO!"

Adding rhyme to haiku, much like deleting seasonal reference, is an innovation Emanuel has made in his haiku. He has attempted to widen the sensory impact of haiku beyond the effect of the single impression given in a traditional haiku. Jazz is not only an expression of African American individualism, but it also inspires African Americans into cooperation and dialogue. A series of haiku under the title "Jazz as Chopsticks" feature the unity and cooperation of two individuals. The first haiku in the series reads,

> If Twin's the arrow,
> Chops plays bow. No JAZZ fallin'
> if they both don't go.

(82)

As does this one, the rest of the haiku, "Chops Makes Drum Sounds SPIN," "When Stuck on his Lick," and "Chops, Whatcha Doin'?" (82) describe jazz performance in terms of a pair of chopsticks. In his notes Emanuel remarks, "Chops and Twin are names given to the chopsticks (Chops the slower, sturdier one, Twin the roaming, more imaginative one)" (82). The pair play the roles of bow and arrow: if they do not work together, they fall and fail to capture what they desire. The pair are in unison with the music, Chops making "drum sounds SPIN" and Twin coaxing them, herding them in. Jazz would not be inspirational if only one individual played the music: Chops's role is as important as Twin's. Jazz captures life as though the pair "harpoons the whale"; while "Chops runs the scale," "Twin slides loose." And jazz music intensifies with a coordination of bass and melody, a pair of chopsticks.

Emanuel's admonition for African Americans to be individualistic in their lives is remindful of Zen doctrine. The concept of subjectivity in Zen, however, goes a step further, for it calls for a severe critique of self.

The doctrine of satori calls for the follower to annihilate self to reach the higher state of *mu*, so as to liberate self from the habitual way of life. In Zen, one must destroy not only self-centeredness and intellectualism, but also God, Buddha, Christ, any prophet, or any idol—because it is only the self, no one else, who can deliver the individual to the state of *mu*. Emanuel urges the liberation of self and the destruction of injustice in such jazz haiku as "Jackhammer," "Ammunition," and "Impressionist" (70). Each piece focuses on the sound of jazz that inspires the liberation of self from the ways one has been conditioned to lead. In "Jackhammer," Emanuel argues that jazz pounds away the door of racism: "Jackhammer Jazz POUNDS— / just breathes—on your door. Message: / don't lock it no more" (70). In "Ammunition," Emanuel observes that jazz is an ammunition to destroy barbarism: people will "fall, rise hypnotized / maybe civilized" (70). "Impressionist" shows that through its impressionist pipe, jazz creates "brightsoapbubbling air," a colorful, exciting new world.

The liberation of self that jazz inspires is akin to the concept of liberation in Zen. Zen teaches its followers to liberate themselves from human laws, rules, and authorities. For jazz, as for Zen, liberation results from one's desire to adhere to the law and spirit of nature. In a haiku on "The Rabbit Capers," which resembles a *senryu*,[9]

> White Bugsy Rabbit
> went scratch-scratch-scratch: jailed for theft
> from The Old Jazz Patch.
>
> (78)

the jazz caper is portrayed as a work of art that is created for its own sake: the jazzrabbit, in another haiku, "aims his gun, shoots / . . . just for fun" (78). For Emanuel, jazz inspires one, as does Zen, with a new way of life: jazz and Zen admonish one to purge one's mind and heart of any materialistic thoughts and feelings, and appreciate the wonder of life here and now.

4

In portraying the union of humanity and nature, the haiku poet must achieve its effect by expressing the feeling of unity and harmony. Based on Zen philosophy, such feelings are motivated by a desire to perceive the harmony of nature and human life, an intuition that nothing is alone nothing is out of the ordinary. The famous haiku by Basho below, quoted earlier, expresses the unity and relatedness in human life:

Autumn is deepening:
What does the neighbor do
For a living?[10]

On a journey Basho rested in a lodge where he saw another traveler, a stranger, staying overnight. As he was reminded of an autumnal self, he was also concerned about the other person. Because he did not come from a well-to-do family, his life as an artist was that of a wandering bard who was enormously interested in commonplace and the common people.

Like Basho's haiku, many of Emanuel's haiku also express genuine feelings about his fellow human beings. Like Whitman's "Song of Myself," the dominant voice recorded in Emanuel's jazz haiku, "John Coltrane," for example, is that of the common people:

"Love Supreme," JA-A-Z train,
tops. Prompt lightning-express, but
made ALL local stops.

                                                                (24)

The three jazz haiku under the title "The Middle Passage"— "Tight-bellied Ships, Gorged," "Chains, Whips, Ship-to-Shore," and "Chain-mates, Black, Vomit" (74)—depict the pain and suffering of fellow human beings as poignantly as do the prose of Toni Morrison's *Beloved* and Charles Johnson's *The Middle Passage*.

In emphasizing "the toughness of poverty and racial injustice" in African American life, Emanuel at times uses narrative style and rhyme. Not only do these haiku on the Middle Passage capture the epitome of racial injustice, Emanuel is also able to intensify his vision in a painful narrative as he is not in a single haiku. All the same, his narrative haiku are endowed with natural, universal sentiments, as they are not motivated by social or political protests. The feelings expressed in Emanuel's haiku transcend those of the individual or society; they are nature-centered sentiments, not even human-centered emotions. Limiting each of the haiku to a single impression, as he has attempted to do, he is able to avoid overly intellectualized or moralized reasoning.

One of the poetic sensibilities that characterize haiku is *wabi*. The expression of *wabi* in classic haiku is characterized by the feelings of agedness, leanness, and coldness, as well as poverty. Some poets are inspired by the sentiment that human beings desire beauty more than food, a sensibility animals do not possess. Richard Wright, too, composed haiku that reflect the sensibility of *wabi*: for example,

> Merciful autumn
> Tones down the shabby curtains
> Of my rented room.

(Haiku 44)

Wright, while describing his poverty and isolation, intimates the transcendence of materialism and the creation of beauty. Wright captures the beauties of nature represented by various images, such as the setting sun in "That abandoned house, / With its yard of fallen leaves, / In the setting sun" (*Haiku* 10); one more winter in "In this rented room / One more winter stands outside / My dirty window pane" (*Haiku* 103); one buzzing fly in "This tenement room / In which I sweat this August / Has one buzzing fly" (*Haiku* 106); the moonlight in "I am paying rent / For the lice in my cold room / And the moonlight too" (*Haiku* 115); and the autumn sun in "My decrepit barn / Sags full of self-consciousness / In this autumn sun" (*Haiku* 174). Such beauties of nature compensate for the poet's plight of existence and fulfill his goals as an artist.

As Emanuel's haiku on the blues show, the sensibility of *wabi* also underlies his poetics. In "Woman's Gone. BLUES Knocks," "No Use Cryin' 'Bout," and "Been Ridin' the Rails" (98), the images of a woman gone, a man crying, and a man riding on a freight train all convey the sensibility of *wabi*, the feelings of loneliness, but the beauty of the blues compensate for such feelings. "Been ridin' the rails," as Emanuel writes in a footnote, refers to "riding freight trains, like a hobo, looking for work in distant towns" (98). He further depicts the toughness of poverty in a long narrative poem, "Sittin'-Log Blues." Despite his unemployment and homelessness, an African American man named Log raises his hopes with toughness and austerity: "I'm standin' kinda crooked, Lord," Log says, "but standin' up is hard to beat" (102–3).

This perspective in viewing pain, poverty, and loneliness in light of their compensation creates paradox. As Emily Dickinson's view of failure is paradoxical in such a poem as her "Success Is Counted Sweetest" (*Complete Poems* 35), Emanuel's narrative poem "The Knockout Blues" expresses paradox. An African American finds his poverty compensated for by the strength of his character in winning the battle of life: "Willin' to work for a wage less than fair, / I couldn't find nothin' but a knockout stare" (104). Despite the racial prejudice rampant in American society, the hero of the poem is proud to say,

> If my arms and legs is wobbly,
> if my neck is leanin' in,
> I been fightin' what I couldn't see
> in places wasn't worth bein' in.

(105)

"The Downhill Blue" also resounds with paradox. The poet-narrator is least afraid of going downhill, because "They say I'm tough with steerin' wheels / and mighty sharp with brakes" (106). "But whatever's below's," he observes, is too deep for a spineless man to fathom. Endowed with character and discipline that have guided his life, he is now prepared to meet the challenge. With a bit of humor, he imagines that as he digs deeper he will end up on the other side of the earth: "when I break through I'll be a Chinese man. / If the earth be's round the way they say, / when I come up it'll be a OPPOSITE day. / Downhill's a long, long way to go, / but I can dig it if I dig it slow. / I'll turn up talkin' in a Chinese way: / servin' up the blues on a thank-you tray" (107).[11] "The Downhill Blues" also suggests that Emanuel's poetic experiment is an attempt to gauge African American life from a nonwestern, cross-cultural point of view.

Such ideas of compensation and paradox enable Emanuel to focus on the creation of beauty in his jazz haiku. A haiku on Billie Holiday,

> Hurt, always hurt. Wounds
> bled wounds, scarred stand-up power:
> this worn, sad flower.

(46)

celebrates a state of mind similar to *wabi*. Despite, and because of, the wounds, "this worn, sad flower" is strengthened by its "stand-up power." This haiku not only expresses a poetic enlightenment but also delineates the beauty of a flower, a symbol of nature. The focus in the rest of the haiku on Billie Holiday, "Wrong Arms to Sleep on" and "Domino Lovers" (46), is on the beauty of nature as well. While such images as "one rose" and "the frost set in" brighten up the feelings of pain and hardship, they also remain beautiful by themselves. In the haiku "Sonny Rollins (Under the Williamsburg Bridge)," Emanuel depicts a lone-wolf in flight as a thing of beauty:

Worldwaif: lone-wolf notes,
blown in pain with all his might,
heal themselves in flight.

(54)

For an African American artist, not only does nature heal the artist's
wounds, but also it creates a powerful image of beauty.

Jazz, as Emanuel remarks in his preface, "has crossed oceans and
continents to spread its gospel of survival through joy and artistic imagination" (v). Throughout *Jazz from the Haiku King*, he is
intent on composing haiku on the basis of its well-established philosophical and aesthetic principles. Philosophically, his finely wrought
haiku enlighten the reader as inspiring jazz does the listener. Aesthetically as well, Emanuel's haiku, sharing the devices of both
haiku and jazz by which to seize the moments of revelation, express
natural, spontaneous sentiments. His haiku, with sharp, compressed
images, strongly reflect the syncopated sounds and rhythms of African American Jazz.

NOTES

CHAPTER 1

1. The translations of this verse and other Japanese poems quoted in this book, unless otherwise noted, are by Hakutani.
2. Donald Keene notes, "The humor in *Chikuba Kyōgin Shū* has been characterized as 'tepid.' The same might be said of the haikai poetry composed by Arakida Moritake (1473–1549), a Sinto priest from the Great Shrine at Ise who turned from serious to comic renga late in life, and has been customarily styled (together with Sōkan) as a founder of haikai no renga" (Keene 13–14).
3. A certain group of poets, including Ito Shintoku (1634–98) and Ikenishi Gonsui (1650–1722) of the Teitoku school, and Uejima Onitsura (1661–1738), Konishi Raizan (1654–1716), and Shiinomoto Saimaro (1656–1738), of the Danrin school, each contributed to refining Basho's style (Keene 56–57).
4. A detailed historical account of *haikai* poetry is given in Keene 337–57.
5. The original of "A Morning Glory" is quoted from Fujio Akimoto, *Haiku Nyumon* 23.
6. The original of "Were My Wife Alive" is quoted from Akimoto (200).
7. The original of "The Harvest Moon" is quoted from "Meigetsu | ya | tatami-no | ue | ni | matsu-no-kage" (Henderson 58).
8. Waley further shows with Zeami's works that the aesthetic principle of *yugen* originated from Zen Buddhism. "It is obvious," Whaley writes, "that Seami [Zeami] was deeply imbued with the teachings of Zen, in which cult Yoshimitsu may have been his master" (*Nō Plays of Japan* 21–22).
9. See Max Loehr, *The Great Paintings of China* 216.
10. The originals of both haiku are quoted from Henderson 160.
11. The original is quoted from Henderson 164.
12. The original is quoted from Akimoto 222.
13. The original is quoted from Blyth, *History* 2: 322.

CHAPTER 2

1. The translation of this haiku is by Noguchi, in *Selected English Writings of Yone Noguchi* 2: 73–74. Translations of other haiku quoted in this chapter are by R. H. Blyth unless otherwise noted.

2. The original is quoted from Henderson 49. The translation of this haiku, "How Cool It Is!" is by Hakutani.

3. Quoted and translated by Keene 93.

4. Haruo Shirane notes, "Bashō worked to assimilate the Chinese and Japanese poetic traditions into haikai and to appropriate the authority and aura of the ancients—whose importance grew in the late seventeenth century, as exemplified by the ancient studies of Confucian texts by Itō Jinsai (1627–1705) and the ancient studies of the *Man'yōshū* by Keichū (1640–1701). As we have seen, Bashō incorporated orthodox Neo-Confucian thought into haikai poetics, hoping to raise the status of haikai, give it a spiritual and cosmological backbone, and make it part of the larger poetic and cultural tradition" (289).

5. This analects is remindful of John Keats's line "Beauty is truth, truth beauty" in "Ode on a Grecian Urn" (1819). Emily Dickinson personifies beauty and truth in her poem "I Died for Beauty—but Was Scarce." Dickinson sees Beauty and Truth united in life and death:

> He questioned softly, "Why I failed"?
> "For Beauty", I replied—
> "And I—for Truth—Themself are One—
> We Brethren, are", He said—
> And so, as Kinsmen, met a Night—
> We talked between the Rooms—
> Until the Moss had reached our lips—
> And covered up—our names—
>
> (*Complete Poems* 216)

6. As his first book, *A Week on the Concord and Merrimack Rivers* (1849), indicates, Thoreau was fascinated with Buddhism. "It is necessary not to be Christian," Thoreau argued, "to appreciate the beauty and significance of the life of Christ. I know that some will have hard thoughts of me, when they hear their Christ named beside my Buddha, yet I am sure that I am willing they should love their Christ more than my Buddha" (*A Week* 67).

7. Walt Whitman, who was also influenced by Buddhism, wrote in "Song of Myself":

> I am the poet of the Body and I am the poet of the Soul,
> The pleasures of heaven are with me and the pains of
>   hell are with me,
> . . . .
> I am the poet of the woman the same as the man.
>
> (*Complete Poetry* 39)

8. As noted earlier, *wabi* underlies the uniquely human perception of beauty derived from poverty. Referring to Basho's aesthetic principle, R. H. Blyth observes, "Without contact with the things, with cold and hunger, real poetry is impossible. Further, Bashō was a missionary spirit and knew that all over Japan were people capable of treading the Way of Haiku. But beyond this, just as with Christ, Bashō's heart was turned towards poverty and simplicity; it was his fate, his lot, his destiny as a poet" (*Haiku* 296).

9. According to R H. Blyth, Zen "means that state of mind in which we are not separated from other things, are indeed identical with them, and yet retain our own individuality and personal peculiarities, . . . it means a body of experience and practice begun by Daruma (who came to China 520 A. D.) as the practical application to living of Mahayana doctrines, and continued to the present day in Zen temples and Zen books of instruction" (*Haiku* 5).

10. While R. H. Blyth observed that an image in haiku does not function as a metaphor, Haruo Shirane argues that "haikai, like all poetry, is highly metaphorical: the essential difference, as we shall see, is that the metaphorical function is implicit rather than stated and often encoded in a polysemous phrase or word" (Shirane 46).

11. As pointed out in the introduction, Yeats was a symbolist poet, whereas Pound took pride in being an Imagist poet. Yeats considered himself a symbolist poet since he was fascinated by the *noh* play, which displays on the stage a painted old pine tree, for example, as a symbol of eternity rather than a scene of landscape, an image of nature. Pound, on the other hand, advocated creation of images rather than symbols in composing poetry.

CHAPTER 3

1. Much of Yone Noguchi's biographical information is found in the autobiographical essays written in English and in Japanese. The most useful is a collection of such essays titled *The Story of Yone Noguchi Told by Himself* (London: Chatto & Windus, 1914).

2. That Poe's poems made a great impact on the aspiring poet from Japan is indicated by the close similarity in a certain part of "Lines," one of Noguchi's early poems in English, and Poe's "Eulalie." See "Lines," in *Pilgrimage* 2: 79; and "Eulalie," Poe, *Complete Works of Poe* 1: 121–22. When Noguchi's poems, including "Lines," appeared in *The Lark*, *The Chap Book*, and *The Philistine*, in 1896, he was accused of plagiarism by some critics while he was defended by his friends. Noguchi later refuted it in *Story of Yone Noguchi* 18. About this controversy, see Don B. Graham, "Yone Noguchi's 'Poe Mania.'"

3. *The American Diary of a Japanese Girl* was published by Frank Leslie Publishing House, New York, in 1901 and also by Frederick A. Stokes Company, New York, in 1902. Both editions are illustrated in color and black and white by Genjiro Yeto. This book was later expanded into a

full novel under the same title. Cf. *The American Diary of a Japanese Girl* (Tokyo: Fuzanbo and London: Elkin Mathews, 1902). This novel has recently been republished: Yone Noguchi, *The Diary of a Japanese Girl*, ed. Edward Marx and Laura E. Franey, with original illustrations by Genjiro Yeto (Philadelphia: Temple University Press, 2007).

4. The most comprehensive, though often inaccurate, bibliography of Yone Noguchi's writings in Japanese and in English is included in Usaburo Toyama, ed., *Essays on Yone Noguchi*, vol. 1.

5. See Noguchi, *Collected English Letters*, ed. Ikuko Atsumi, 210–11.

6. Yone Noguchi had earlier met Yeats in London, where *From the Eastern Sea* was published in 1903. In a letter of February 24, 1903, to his wife, Leonie Gilmour, he wrote, "I made many a nice young, lovely, kind friend among literary *geniuses* (attention!). W. B. Yeats or Laurence Binyon, Moore and Bridges. They are so good; they invite me almost everyday. They are jolly companions. Their hairs are not long, I tell you" (*Collected English Letters* 106).

7. See Isamu Noguchi, *A Sculptor's World* 31.

8. See Yone Noguchi, "The Invisible Night," *Seen and Unseen* 21. The poem first appeared in *The Lark*. The poem is quoted from *Selected English Writings* 1: 65.

9. See "At the Yuigahama Shore by Kamakura," *Pilgrimage* 1: 34. The poem is reprinted in Noguchi's travelogue *Kamakura* 38–39.

10. See *Story of Noguchi* 223–24. Noguchi discusses elsewhere what is to him the true meaning of realism: "While I admit the art of some artist which has the detail of beauty, I must tell him that reality, even when true, is not the whole thing; he should learn the art of escaping from it. That art is, in my opinion, the greatest of all arts; without it, art will never bring us the eternal and the mysterious" (*Spirit of Japanese Art* 103).

11. Quoted, in Noguchi's translation, in *Spirit of Japanese Poetry* 38.

12. Quoted in *Spirit of Japanese Poetry* 37. This particular poem, however, cannot be found in any of Noguchi's poetry collections.

13. Quoted, in Noguchi's translation, in Noguchi, *Through the Torii* 132.

14. See "By the Engakuji Temple: Moon Night," *Pilgrimage* 1: 5. The Engakuji Temple, located in Kamakura, an ancient capital of Japan, was founded in the thirteenth century by Tokimune Hojo, hero of the feudal government who was a great believer in Zen Buddhism.

15. See Charles Warren Stoddard, "Introduction," *Voice of the Valley* 10–11.

CHAPTER 4

1. Earl Miner, in *Japanese Tradition*, closely examines Yeats's relationship to the *noh* play and also discusses Yeats's association with Ezra Pound with respect to East-West literary relations. But Miner does not consider Yone Noguchi in this context. Makoto Ueda's *Zeami, Basho, Yeats, Pound* does not mention Noguchi. Nor does Liam Miller's *Noble Drama*

of Yeats, which includes well-annotated analyses of Yeats's *noh* plays in comparison with the Japanese model, mention Noguchi.

2. Among the East-West comparative critics, Roy E. Teele is the one who demonstrates Fenollosa's failure to understand the Japanese language, particularly the essential rhythm of the *noh* text Fenollosa translated. See Teele's "Japanese Translations."

3. For a discussion of Noguchi's English poetry and literary criticism, see Hakutani, "Noguchi's Poetry."

4. *The Egoist* was one of the prestigious literary magazines published in London in the 1910s. When Noguchi contributed two of his articles to the magazine, its assistant editor was T. S. Eliot.

5. This lecture was published as "Chapter II: The Japanese Hokku Poetry" in Noguchi's *Spirit of Japanese Poetry* 33–53.

6. This lecture was published as "Japanese Poetry" in *Transactions* 12: 86–109.

7. See *Hiroshige.* This book was followed by other books on Japanese painting: *Korin, Utamaro, Hokusai, Harunobu,* and *Ukiyoye Primitives.*

8. A unifying image or action appears frequently in Yeats's *noh* plays as it does in Japanese *noh* plays. The well choked up with leaves in *At the Hawk's Well* is represented by a piece of cloth that remains throughout the performance just as the bed-ridden lady Aoi no Ue, the heroine of the *noh* play *Aoi no Ue,* is symbolized by a sleeve laid on the stage during the performance. In Yeats's *The Dreaming of the Bones,* the young girl's spirit speaks impersonally of herself as the old man and the old woman in the *noh* play *Nishikigi,* in Pound's version, speak in unison. The climactic dance of the Rainbow Skirt and Feather Jacket performed in Noguchi's *noh* play "The Everlasting Sorrow" is also a unified image since it symbolizes the flight of two birds with one wing.

9. See Noguchi's "Everlasting Sorrow," in which the Sovereign Ming Huang longs for the earthly return of his mistress Yang Kue-fei, who has long departed for Heaven. A Taoist priest is commanded by the Sovereign to find the lady Bang's lost soul. Upon finding her, the priest asks her to give a token as proof of his meeting with her. Though she offers her hairpin to take back with him, he declines it as too common and asks her to present something special that Ming Huang would remember as belonging to her alone. "In deep," Yang Kuei-fei responds, "I now happen to recall to my mind how on the seventh day of the seventh moon, in the Hall of Immortality, at midnight when no one was anear." Then the chorus sings, "the Sovereign whispered in my ears, after pledging the two stars in the sky:

> In heaven we will ever fly like one-winged birds;
> On earth grow joined like a tree with branches
>   twining tight."

At the climax of the play, Yang Kuei-fei performs for the priest a dance of the Rainbow Skirt and Feather Jacket to convey Ming Huang "the dancer's heart." Noguchi adds a note: "Each bird must fly with a mate, since it has only one wing" (142).

10. One of the players who made an indispensable contribution to Yeats's understanding of *noh* performance was a Japanese dancer, Michio Itoh. He came from a distinguished family of theater artists. Two of his brothers, Kensaku Itoh and Koreya Senda, who also distinguished themselves in the theater in Japan as late as after World War II, are both famous for their work as stage designers and as dancers. The papier-mâché mask Itoh wore for the performance of *At the Hawk's Well* in 1926 was made by Isamu Noguchi, the son of Yone Noguchi and his American wife, Leonie Gilmour (Isamu Noguchi, *Sculptor's World* 123). The performance of the play demanded in its music, movement, and visual effect, firsthand knowledge of the *noh* theater. It was Pound who introduced Itoh to Yeats, who thought Itoh's "minute intensity of movement in the dance of the hawk so well suited our small room and private art" (*Plays of Yeats* 417).

11. In the play a fisherman finds on a pine tree a feather robe that belongs to a fair angel. She begs him to return the robe and offers to dance for him in return. He insists on keeping the robe with him until she completes her dance. She assures him that angels never break promises, saying that falsehood exists only among mortals. The fisherman, deeply ashamed, hands back the robe to her. The angel, completing her performance, vanishes into the air.

12. For Pound's and Fenollosa's version, see Pound and Fenollosa, *Classic Noh Theatre* 98–104.

13. In the play, the Mountain Elf during the night circles round the mountain, a symbol of life. At the climax a famous dancer, another elf who has lost her way in the Hill of Shadow on her way to the Holy Buddhist Temple appears and inquires the right road of the Mountain Elf "with large star-like eyes and fearful snow-white hair." The Mountain Elf then shows the dancer how to encircle the mountain (*Spirit of Japanese Poetry* 66–67).

CHAPTER 5

1. See Miner, "Pound, *Haiku* and the Image" 570–84; and *Japanese Tradition*. There is some ambiguity in Miner's chronology since, in his article, the date of Pound's joining the Poets' Club is said to be "just before the first World War," which means perhaps between 1913 and 1914 ("Pound" 572). There is also another ambiguity with respect to the time and circumstance of Pound's learning about "the usefulness of Japanese poetry from Flint." Flint's interest in Japanese poetry is indicated in his own account of the matter, published in *The Egoist* for May 1, 1915: "I had been advocating in the course of a series of articles on recent books

of verse a poetry in *vers libre*, akin in spirit to the Japanese" (*Japanese Tradition* 100).

2. For Noguchi's life and work, see Hakutani, ed. *Selected English Writings of Yone Noguchi: An East-West Literary Assimilation*, vol. 1: *Poetry* (1990) and vol. 2: *Prose* (1992). For a study of Noguchi's life, including an interview with his son, American sculptor Isamu Noguchi, see Hakutani, "Father and Son: A Conversation with Isamu Noguchi." For a discussion of Noguchi's English poetry and literary criticism, see Hakutani, "Yone Noguchi's Poetry: From Whitman to Zen."

3. The impact of *hokku* on Pound was apparently greater and more beneficial than that on his fellow Imagists. Regarding the form of superposition as ideal for expressing instantaneous perception, Pound wrote in a footnote, "Mr. Flint and Mr. Rodker have made longer poems depending on a similar presentation of matter. So also have Richard Aldington, in his *In Via Sestina*, and 'H. D.' in her *Oread*, which latter poems express much stronger emotions than that in my lines here given" ("Vorticism" 467). Pound's argument here suggests that *hokku* and Pound's *hokku*-like poems can express instantaneous and spontaneous perception better than can the longer poems and the poems with stronger emotions.

4. See Noguchi, "What Is a Hokku Poem?" *Rhythm* 11 (January 1913): 354–59. The essay was reprinted in Noguchi's *Through the Torii* 126–39. The page numbers cited hereafter refer to the *Rhythm* version.

5. In a letter of November 24, 1913, to Pound, Mary Fenollosa wrote, "I am beginning with [*sic*] right now, to send you material." On the following day she wrote again, "Please don't get discouraged at the ragged way this manuscript is coming to you. As I said yesterday, it will all get there in time,—which is the most important thing." See Kodama, ed. *Ezra Pound and Japan: Letters and Essays* 6.

6. One of Pound's critics who acknowledge this fact, Roy E. Teele, demonstrates Fenollosa's failure to understand the Japanese language, particularly the essential rhythm of the *noh* text Fenollosa translated. See Teele, "The Japanese Translations" 61–66.

7. Earl Miner, who states that Pound knew nothing about Japanese poetry before 1913 or 1914, believes that Pound later learned about *hokku* in the writings of the French translators ("Pound" 572–73).

8. See Noguchi, "The Everlasting Sorrow: A Japanese Noh Play" 141–43 and "The Japanese Noh Play" 99.

9. Noguchi first met Yeats in 1903 as indicated in a letter Noguchi wrote to Leonie Gilmour, his first wife: "I made many a nice young, lovely, kind friend among literary *genius* (attention!) W. B. Yeats or Laurence Binyon, Moore and Bridges. They are so good; they invite me almost every day" (Noguchi, *Collected English Letters* 106). In 1921 Yeats, who was in Oxford, England, sent a long letter to Noguchi, who was in Japan, and wrote, in part, in reference to art and poetry, "The old French poets were simple as the modern are not, & I find in Francois Villon the same

thoughts, with more intellectual power, that I find in the Gaelic poet [Raftery]. I would be simple myself but I do not know how. I am always turning over pages like those you have sent me, hoping that in my old age I may discover how. . . . A form of beauty scarcely lasts a generation with us, but it lasts with you for centuries. You no more want to change it than a pious man wants to change the Lord's Prayer, or the Crucifix on the wall [blurred] at least not unless we have infected you with our egotism" (*Collected English Letters* 220–21).

10. See William Pratt, *The Imagist Poem* 14–15; J. B. Harmer, *Victory in Limbo: Imagism 1908–1917* 17; Humphrey Carpenter, *A Serious Character: The Life of Ezra Pound* 115.

11. It is speculative, of course, but quite possible that Aldington, fascinated by Japanese visual arts, might have read the three articles about the subject Noguchi published in this period: "Utamaro," *Rhythm* 11, no. 10 (November 1912): 257–60; "Koyetsu," *Rhythm* 11, no. 11 (December 1912): 302–5; "The Last Master [Yoshitoshi] of the Ukiyoye School," *The Transactions of the Japan Society of London* 12 (April 1914): 144–56. Moreover, *The Spirit of Japanese Art* (1915) includes chapters on major Japanese painters such as Koyetsu, Kenzan, Kyosai, and Busho Hara, besides Utamaro and Hiroshige. If Aldington had read these essays, he would very well have been acquainted with Noguchi's writings about Japanese poetics.

12. Aldington's poem reads,

> The apparition of these poems in a crowd:
> White faces in a black dead faint.

See Aldington, "Penultimate Poetry," *Egoist* (15 January 1915). This poem sounds more like *senryu*, a humorous haiku, than the *hokku* Pound was advocating. *Senryu* originated from Karai Senryu, an eighteenth-century Japanese haiku poet.

13. See Davie, *Ezra Pound* 42 and Carpenter 247.

14. See Toyama, ed., *Essays on Yone Noguchi* (mostly in Japanese) 1: 327.

15. See Jones, *Life and Opinions of Hulme* 122. Neither Noel Stock in *Poet in Exile: Ezra Pound* nor Humphrey Carpenter in *Serious Character* mentions Pound's activities at the Quest Society, let alone Pound's possible interactions with Noguchi.

16. See T. S. Eliot's introduction to *Literary Essays of Ezra Pound* 23.

17. About this time Noguchi also wrote an essay titled "A Japanese Note on Yeats," included in his book of essays, *Through the Torii* 110–17.

18. Noguchi's "Tell Me the Street to Heaven" was first published in his essay "What Is a Hokku Poem?" *Rhythm* 11 (January 1913): 358, as indicated earlier, and reprinted in *Through the Torii* (1914 and 1922). The other *hokku*, "Is It, Oh, List" was also included in the same issue and reprinted in *Through the Torii* with a change in the third line: "So runs Thames, so runs my Life" (136).

19. The original in Japanese reads "Hiya-hiya to / Kabe wo fumaete / Hirune kana." See Henderson 49. The English translation of this haiku is by Hakutani.

20. Alan Durant tries to show that Pound's metro poem linguistically contains a number of metaphors and associations, and that it is not as imagistic as critics say. While Durant's interpretation is valid as far as the various elements in the poem appear to the reader as metaphors and associations, Pound's intention does differ from the reader's interpretation. The same thing may occur in the interpretation of a Japanese *hokku*, but traditionally the language of the *hokku*, as Noguchi demonstrates throughout *The Spirit of Japanese Poetry*, shuns metaphor and symbolism. See Alan Durant, "Pound, Modernism and Literary Criticism: A Reply to Donald Davie."

21. This passage is quoted from "Again on *Hokku*," included in *Through the Torii* 140–46. A *verbatim* account is given in the introduction to his *Japanese Hokkus* 22–23. For Noguchi's London experiences, see "My First London Experience (1903)" and "Again in London (1913–14)" in *Story of Yone Noguchi* 119–65.

22. The union of different experiences is reminiscent of T. S. Eliot's statement about an amalgamation. In reference to John Donne's poetry, Eliot writes, "When a poet's mind is perfectly equipped for its work, it is constantly amalgamating disparate experience; the ordinary man's experience is chaotic, irregular, fragmentary. The latter falls in love, or reads Spinoza, and these two experiences have nothing to do with each other, or with the noise of the typewriter or the smell of cooking; in the mind of the poet these experiences are always forming new wholes" (*Selected Essays* 247).

23. In *The Spirit of Japanese Poetry*, Noguchi wrote, "As the so-called literary expression is a secondary matter in the realm of poetry, there is no strict boundary between the domains generally called subjective and objective; while some *Hokku* poems appear to be objective, those poems are again by turns quite subjective through the great virtue of the writers having the fullest identification with the matter written on. You might call such collation poetical trespassing; but it is the very point whence the Japanese poetry gains unusual freedom; that freedom makes us join at once with the soul of Nature" (43–44).

24. To the Japanese, such expressions as "the light of passion" and "the cicada's song" immediately evoke images of hot summer. These phrases in Japanese are attributed to or closely associated with summer; cicada is a *kigo* for summer.

25. For Whitman's influence on Noguchi, see Chapter 3.

CHAPTER 6

1. In *A Week on the Concord and Merrimack Rivers* (1849), Thoreau wrote, "We can tolerate all philosophies, Atomists, Pneumatologists, Atheists, Theists,— Plato, Aristotle, Leucippus, Democritus, Pythagoras,

Zoroaster and Confucius. It is the attitude of these men, more than any communication which they make, that attracts us" (152). In the conclusion of *Variorum Civil Disobedience*, Thoreau evoked Confucius: "The progress from an absolute to a limited monarchy, from a limited monarchy to a democracy, is a progress toward a true respect for the individual. Even the Chinese philosopher was wise enough to regard the individual as the basis of the empire" (*Variorum Civil Disobedience* 55).

2. John Tytell observes, "Kerouac . . . attacked the concept of revision sacred to most writers as a kind of secondary moral censorship imposed by the unconscious" (*Naked Angels* 17).

3. In *The Dharma Bums*, Kerouac saw human existence as a strange beetle when he climbed Mount Hozomeen: "Standing on my head before bedtime on that rock roof of the moonlight I could indeed see that the earth was truly upsidedown and man a weird vain beetle full of strange ideas walking around upsidedown and boasting, and I could realize that man remembered why this dream of planets and plants and Plantagenets was built out of the primordial essence" (187).

4. As noted earlier, Pound quoted Moritake's haiku just before discussing the often-quoted poem "In a Station of the Metro": "The apparition of these faces in the crowd: / Petals, on a wet, black bough" ("Vorticism" 48).

5. Like Thoreau, Kerouac grew up a Christian and was well versed in the Bible but became fascinated with Buddhism. "It is necessary not to be Christian," he argued, "to appreciate the beauty and significance of the life of Christ. I know that some will have hard thoughts of me, when they hear their Christ named beside my Buddha, yet I am sure that I am willing they should love their Christ more than my Buddha" (*A Week* 67).

6. Evoking his mother in his meditation has an affinity with Whitman's allusion to the old mother in "Out of the Cradle Endlessly Rocking":

> The aria sinking,
> All else continuing, the stars shining,
> The winds blowing, the notes of the bird continuous echoing,
> With angry moans the fierce old mother incessantly moaning,

> (*Complete Poetry* 183)

7. In *The Dharma Bums*, as Kerouac hitchhiked home to see his mother in North Carolina, he thought of her and Gary Snyder. Kerouac wrote about Snyder, "Why is he so mad about white tiled sinks and 'kitchen machinery' he calls it?" Referring to his mother's doing the dishes in the white sink, Kerouac remarked, "People have good hearts whether or not they live like Dharma Bums. Compassion is the heart of Buddhism" (105). At the end of his journey to Mount Hozomeen, Kerouac witnessed "the world was upsidedown hanging in an ocean of endless

space and here were all these people sitting in theaters watching movies. . . . Pacing in the yard at dusk, singing 'Wee Small Hours,' when I came to the lines 'when the whole wide world is fast asleep' my eyes filled with tears, 'Okay world,' I said, 'I'll love ya.' In bed at night, warm and happy in my bag on the good hemp bunk, I'd see my table and my clothes in the moonlight . . . and on this I'd go to sleep like a lamb" (187–88).

8. *Walden* teaches the virtue of drinking pure water, for drinking tea, coffee, wine, or smoking tobacco or opium would harm not only one's physical health but one's mental health: "I believe that water is the only drink for a wise man; wine is not so noble a liquor; and think of dashing the hopes of a morning with a cup of warm coffee, or of an evening with a dish of tea! Ah, how low I fall when I am tempted by them!" (217).

9. Melville writes, "Is it that by its indefiniteness it shadows forth the heartless voids and immensities of the universe, and thus stabs us from behind with the thought of annihilation, when beholding the white depths of the milky way? Or is it, that as in essence whiteness is not so much a color as the visible absence of color, and at the same time the concrete of all colors; is it for these reasons that there is such a dumb blankness, full of meaning, in a wide landscape of snows—a colorless, all-color of atheism from which we shrink?" (169).

10. "After Apple-Picking" ends with the lines that intimate having a nightmare, or what Frost calls "just some human sleep" (*Frost's Poems* 229).

11. See the last stanza in Poem 449 "I Died for Beauty" and 712 "Because I Could Not Stop for Death" (*Complete Poems* 216, 350).

12. See the last stanza of "The Road Not Taken" (*Frost's Poems* 223).

13. See the lines in "The Weary Blues": "Ain't got nobody in all this world, / Ain't got nobody but ma self"(Hughes, *Selected Poems* 33).

14. See the first two and last two lines in "We Real Cool": "We real cool. We / Left school. We" and "Jazz June. We / Die soon" (Brooks, *Selected Poems* 73).

CHAPTER 7

1. According to Toru Kiuchi, this South African poet, identified as Sinclair Beiles in Michel Fabre's *Richard Wright: Books and Writers* 14, was "one of the Beat poets and . . . his and their interest in Zen led Wright to the knowledge of haiku." Kiuchi further notes that "because the Beat Hotel was in the Latin Quarter and Wright lived very close to the hotel, he must have haunted the hotel bar. I assume that Wright took an interest in Zen, which some of the Beat poets brought up as one of the important topics, and that Wright then must have known haiku through his conversations with Beiles" (Kiuchi's letter to Hakutani).

2. This manuscript consists of a title page and eighty-two pages, page 1 containing the first seven haiku and each of the other pages containing ten, altogether 817 haiku. The manuscript, dated 1960, is in the Wright

collection in the Beinecke Rare Book and Manuscript Library, Yale University, New Haven, Connecticut. The manuscript was published as *Haiku: This Other World*, eds., Yoshinobu Hakutani and Robert L. Tener (New York: Arcade, 1998; New York: Random House, 2000). References to Wright's haiku, including numbers, are to this edition.

3. See the cover of the Random House edition of *Haiku: This Other World*.

4. See Julia Wright, introduction to *Haiku: This Other World* xi.

5. See R. H. Blyth, *Haiku: Eastern Culture* (Tokyo: Hokuseido, 1981). This is a paperback edition of vol. 1 of R. H. Blyth, *Haiku*, 4 vols. (Tokyo: Hokuseido, 1949). Page references to this book are to the 1981 paperback edition.

6. "After the Sermon" can be read as a *senryu*, a subgenre of haiku that expresses humor. Wright might have likened "the preacher's voice" to "the caws of crows," which sound least mellifluous.

7. The original of the haiku is in Henderson 40.

8. The original of the haiku is in Henderson 18. The translation is from Blyth, *History* 2: xxix.

9. The word *sabi*, a noun, derives from the verb *sabiru*, to rust, implying that what is described is aged. *Sabi* is traditionally associated with loneliness. Aesthetically, however, this mode of sensibility intimates of grace rather than splendor; it suggests quiet beauty as opposed to robust beauty. Many of Wright's haiku thrive on the use of the word *lonely*. For further discussion of *sabi* and of other aesthetic principles, see Chapter 1 of this book and Hakutani, *Richard Wright and Racial Discourse* 275–82.

10. The original of Kikaku's haiku is in Henderson 58.

11. The original of Buson's haiku is in Henderson 104.

12. The original of Buson's haiku is in Henderson 102.

CHAPTER 8

1. The original in Japanese reads "Yama-dori-no | o | wo | fumu | haru no | iri-hi | kana" (Henderson 102).

2. The original of this haiku by Basho is in Henderson 40.

3. See *Haiku: This Other World*. The 817 haiku are numbered consecutively, as noted earlier: "In the Silent Forest" is 316 and "A Thin Waterfall" 569.

4. The word *sabi* in Japanese, a noun, derives from the verb *sabiru*, to rust, implying that what is described is aged, as discussed in Chapter 1. Buddha's portrait hung in Zen temples, the old man with a thin body, is nearer to his soul as the old tree with its skin and leaves fallen is nearer to the very origin and essence of nature. For a further discussion of Buddha's portrait, see Loehr 216.

5. As discussed earlier, while Freud defines death as the opposite of life, meaning that death reduces all animate things to the inanimate. Lacan

defines death as "human experience, human interchanges, intersubjectivity," suggesting that death is part of life (*Seminar* 2: 80). To Lacan, the death instinct is not "an admission of impotence, it isn't a coming to a halt before an irreducible, an ineffable last thing, it is a concept" (*Seminar* 2: 70).

6. This stanza, filled with rather superficial racial and cultural labels, is reminiscent of the least inspiring stanza in Whitman's "Song of Myself":

> Magnifying and applying come I,
> Outbidding at the start the old cautious hucksters,
> Taking myself the exact dimensions of Jehovah,
> Lithographing Kronos, Zeus his son, and Hercules
>   his grandson,
> Buying drafts of Osiris, Isis, Belus, Brahma, Buddha,
> In my portfolio placing Manito loose, Allah on a leaf,
>   the crucifix
> engraved,
> With Odin and the hedeous-faced Mexitli and every
>   idol and image,
>
> (Whitman, *Complete Poetry* 58)

CHAPTER 9

1. See "Author's Preface" in *Jazz from the Haiku King* iv.
2. See Chapter 1 of this book, as well as Donald Keene's detailed historical account of *haikai* poetry, from which haiku evolved (337–55).
3. Ellison's essay originally appeared in *Antioch Review* 5 (June 1945): 198–211.
4. As noted in Chapter 1, the first collection of *renga*, *Chikuba Kyogin Shu* (*Chikuba Singers' Collection*, 1499) includes over two hundred *tsukeku* (adding verses) linked with the first verses of another poet. As the title of the collection suggests, the salient characteristic of *renga* was a display of ingenuity and coarse humor.
5. Craig Werner has provided an incisive account of the jazz impulse: "Jazz, observed Louis Armstrong, is music that's never played the same way twice. The world changes, the music changes. Jazz imagines the transitions, distills the deepest meanings of the moment we're in, how it developed from the ones that came before, how it opens up into the multiple possibilities of the ones to come" (*Change* 132).
6. In "A Sight in Camp in the Daybreak Gray and Dim" (*Complete Poetry* 219), an elegy for the dead soldiers, Whitman celebrates their death and alludes to their natural and divine heritage.
7. Thomas Jefferson's *Notes on the State of Virginia* (1785) has a passage revealing his basic attitude toward nature and humanity: "Those who

labour in the earth are the chosen people of God, if ever he had a chosen people, whose breasts he has made his peculiar deposit for substantial and genuine virtue" (164–65).

8. For the origin and development of this verse form, see Keene 109–15.

9. *Senryu*, as noted earlier, is a humorous haiku. *Senryu* as a poetic genre thrives on moralizing nuances and a philosophical tone that expresses the incongruity of things rather than their oneness. Because *senryu* tend to appeal more to one's sense of the logical than to intuition, this jazz haiku can be read as a *senryu*.

10. The original of "Autumn Is Deepening" is quoted from Imoto 231.

11. Emanuel's humorous imagination, in which he is dreaming of digging the earth deeper to reach the other side of the world, is reminiscent of Mark Twain's. In *Adventures of Huckleberry Finn*, Tom Sawyer talks about his outrageous far-fetched imagination, in which Jim, imprisoned in the dungeon of the Castle Deep and given a couple of case-knives, would be able to dig himself out through the earth for thirty-seven years and come out in China. Despite Huck's rebuke of Tom for entertaining such an idea, Twain's conjuring up visions of Jim's freedom from slavery to a slaveless society is akin to Emanuel's wish for jazz to cross cultural borders in disseminating the African American suffering and joy. See *Adventures of Huckleberry Finn* 191–92.

WORKS CITED

Akimoto, Fujio. *Haiku Nyumon*. Tokyo: Kodansha, 1971.

Aldington, Richard. "Penultimate Poetry." *Egoist* 15 January 1915.

Blyth, R. H. *Haiku: Eastern Culture*. Tokyo: Hokuseido, 1981.

———. *A History of Haiku*. 2 vols. Tokyo: Hokuseido, 1963, 1964.

Brooks, Gwendolyn. *Selected Poems*. 1963. New York: Harper Perennial, 1999.

Carpenter, Humphrey. *A Serious Character: The Life of Ezra Pound*. Boston: Houghton Mifflin, 1988.

Cather, Willa. "Two Poets: Yone Noguchi and Bliss Carman." *The World and the Parish: Willa Cather's Articles and Reviews, 1893–1902*. 2 vols. Lincoln, NB: University of Nebraska Press, 1970.

Danquah, J. B. *The Akan Doctrine of God: A Fragment of Gold Coast Ethics and Religion*. London: Frank Cass, 1944.

Davie, Donald. *Ezra Pound*. New York: Viking, 1975.

Dickinson, Emily. *The Complete Poems of Emily Dickinson*. Ed. Thomas H. Johnson. Boston: Little, Brown, 1960.

Durant, Alan. "Pound, Modernism and Literary Criticism: A Reply to Donald Davie." *Critical Quarterly* 28 (Spring–Summer 1986): 154–66.

Eliot, T. S. *The Complete Poems and Plays 1909–1950*. New York: Harcourt, Brace & World, 1952.

———. *Selected Essays, 1917–1932*. New York: Harcourt, 1932.

Ellison, Ralph. "Richard Wright's Blues." *Antioch Review* 5 (June 1945): 198–211.

———. *Shadow and Act*. New York: Random House, 1964.

Emanuel, James A. *Jazz from the Haiku King*. Detroit: Broadside, 1999.

Emerson, Ralph Waldo. *Selections from Ralph Waldo Emerson*. Ed. Stephen E. Whicher. Boston: Houghton Mifflin, 1960.

Fabre, Michel. "The Poetry of Richard Wright." *Critical Essays of Richard Wright*. Ed. Yoshinobu Hakutani. Boston: G. K. Hall, 1975. 252–72.

———. *Richard Wright: Books and Writers*. Jackson: University Press of Mississippi, 1990.

———. *The Unfinished Quest of Richard Wright*. New York: Morrow, 1973.

Fenollosa, Ernest. *The Chinese Written Character as a Medium for Poetry*. Ed. Ezra Pound. New York: Arrow, 1936.

Frost, Robert. *Robert Frost's Poems*. Ed. Louis Untermeyer. New York: Pocket Books, 1971.

Gifford, Barry, and Lawrence Lee. *Jack's Book: An Oral Biography of Jack Kerouac*. New York: St. Martin's, 1978.

Goodwin, K. L. *The Influence of Ezra Pound*. London: Oxford University Press, 1966.

Graham, Don B. "Yone Noguchi's 'Poe Mania.'" *Markham Review* 4 (1974): 58–60.

Hakutani, Yoshinobu. "Ezra Pound, Yone Noguchi, and Imagism." *Modern Philology* 90 (August 1992): 46–69.

———. "Father and Son: A Conversation with Isamu Noguchi." *Journal of Modern Literature* 42 (Summer 1990): 13–33.

———. *Richard Wright and Racial Discourse*. Columbia: University of Missouri Press, 1996.

———. "Richard Wright's Haiku, Zen, and the African 'Primal Outlook upon Life.'" *Modern Philology* 104 (May 2007): 510–28.

———. "Yone Noguchi's Poetry: From Whitman to Zen." *Comparative Literature Studies* 22 (1985): 67–79.

Harmer, J. B. *Victory in Limbo: Imagism 1908–1917*. New York: St. Martin's, 1975.

Henderson, Harold G. *An Introduction to Haiku: An Anthology of Poems and Poets from Basho to Shiki*. New York: Doubleday/Anchor, 1958.

Hughes, Langston. *Selected Poems of Langston Hughes*. New York: Knopf, 1959.

Imoto, Noichi. *Basho: Sono Jinsei to Geijutsu* [*Basho: His Life and Art*]. Tokyo: Kodansha, 1968.

Jefferson, Thomas. *Notes on the State of Virginia*. Ed. William Peden. Chapel Hill: University of North Carolina Press, 1955.

Jones, A. R. *The Life and Opinions of Thomas Ernest Hulme*. Boston: Beacon, 1960.

Jones, Gayl. *Liberating Voices: Oral Tradition in African-American Literature*. Cambridge: Harvard University Press, 1991.

Keene, Donald. *World within Walls: Japanese Literature of the Pre-Modern Era, 1600–1868*. New York: Grove, 1976.

Kenner, Hugh. *The Poetry of Ezra Pound*. Millwood, NY: Kraus, 1947.

Kerouac, Jack. *Book of Haikus*. Ed. Regina Weinreich. New York: Penguin Books, 2003.

———. *The Dharma Bums*. New York: Viking, 1958.

———. "Essentials of Spontaneous Prose." *Evergreen Review* 2 (Summer 1958): 72–73.

———. *On the Road*. New York: Viking, 1958.

Kiuchi, Toru. Letter to Yoshinobu Hakutani on Sinclair Beiles. 7 August 2005.

Kodama, Sanehide., ed. *Ezra Pound and Japan: Letters and Essays*. Redding Ridge, CT: Black Swan Books, 1987.

Kurebayashi, Kodo. *Introduction to Dogen Zen* [in Japanese]. Tokyo: Daihorinkaku, 1983.

Lacan, Jacques. *The Four Fundamental of Concepts of Psychoanalysis*. Ed. Jacques-Alain Miller. Trans. Alan Sheridan. New York: Norton, 1881.

———. *The Seminar of Jacques Lacan*, bk. 2, *The Ego in Freud's Theory and in the Techniques of Psychoanalysis, 1954–1955*. Ed. Jacques-Alain Miller. Trans. Sylvana Tomaselli. New York: Norton, 1988.

Loehr, Max. *The Great Paintings of China*. New York: Harper & Row, 1980.

Lynch, Tom. "Intersecting Influences in American Haiku." *Modernity in East-West Literary Criticism: New Readings*. Ed. Yoshinobu Hakutani. Madison, NJ: Fairleigh Dickinson University Press; London: Associated University Presses, 2001. 114–36.

Melville, Herman. *Moby-Dick*. Ed. Harrison Hayford and Hershel Parker. New York: Norton, 1967.

Miller, Liam. *The Noble Drama of W. B. Yeats*. Dublin: Dolmen, 1977.

Miner, Earl. *The Japanese Tradition in British and American Literature*. Princeton, NJ: Princeton University Press, 1958.

———. "Pound, *Haiku* and the Image." *Hudson Review* 9 (Winter 1957): 570–84.

Morrison, Toni. *Jazz*. New York: Plume, 1993.

Munsterberg, Hugo. *The Arts of Japan: An Illustrated History*. Rutland, VT; Tokyo: Tuttle, 1957.

Noguchi, Isamu. *A Sculptor's World*. New York: Harper & Row, 1968.

Noguchi, Yone. *The American Diary of a Japanese Girl*. New York: Frank Leslie Publishing House, 1901.

———. *Collected English Letters*. Ed. Ikuko Atsumi. Tokyo: Yone Noguchi Society, 1975.

———. *The Diary of a Japanese Girl*. Ed. Edward Marx and Laura E. Franey, with original illustrations by Genjiro Yeto. Philadelphia: Temple University Press, 2007.

———. "The Everlasting Sorrow: A Japanese Noh Play." *Egoist* 4 (1917): 141–43.

———. *From the Eastern Sea*. London: Elkin Mathews, 1903.

———. *Hiroshige*. London: Elkin Mathews, 1921.

———. *Japan and America*. Tokyo: Keio University Press, 1921.

———. "The Japanese Noh Play." *Egoist* 5 (1918): 99.

———. "Japanese Poetry." *The Transactions of the Japan Society of London* 12 (1914): 86–109.

———. *Kamakura*. Kamakura: Valley, 1910.

———. *Korin*. London: Elkin Mathews, 1922.

———. "Koyetsu." *Rhythm* 11.11 (December 1912): 302–5.

———. "The Last Master [Yoshitoshi] of the Ukiyoye School." *The Transactions of the Japan Society of London* 12 (April 1914): 144–56.

———. *The Pilgrimage*. 2 vols. Tokyo: Kyobunkan, 1909.

————. *Seen and Unseen or, Monologues of a Homeless Snail*. San Francisco: Burgess & Garnett, 1897.

————. *Selected English Writings of Yone Noguchi: An East-West Literary Assimilation*. Ed. Yoshinobu Hakutani. 2 vols. Rutherford, NJ: Fairleigh Dickinson University Press; London: Associated University Presses, 1990, 1992.

————. *The Spirit of Japanese Art*. New York: Dutton, 1915.

————. *The Spirit of Japanese Poetry*. London: John Murray, 1914.

————. *The Story of Yone Noguchi Told by Himself*. Chatto & Windus, 1914.

————. *The Summer Cloud: Prose Poems*. Tokyo: Shunyodo, 1906.

————. *Through the Torii*. Boston: Four Seas, 1922.

————. *Utamaro*. London: Elkin Mathews, 1923.

————. *The Voice of the Valley*. San Francisco: Doxey, 1897.

————. "What Is a Hokku Poem?" *Rhythm* 11.10 (January 1913): 354–59.

Poe, Edgar Allan. *The Complete Works of Edgar Allan Poe*. Ed. James Albert Harrison. New York: Crowell, 1902.

————. *Selected Writings of Edgar Allan Poe*. Ed. Edward H. Davidson. Boston: Houghton Mifflin, 1956.

Pound, Ezra. "As for Imagisme." *New Age* 14 (1915): 349.

————. *Gaudier-Brzeska: A Memoir*. 1916. New York: New Directions, 1970.

————. *Literary Essays of Ezra Pound*. Ed. and introd. T. S. Eliot. New York: New Directions, 1954.

————. *Personae*. New York: New Directions, 1926.

————. *Selected Poems of Ezra Pound*. New York: New Directions, 1957.

————. *The Spirit of Romance*. New York: New Directions, 1968.

————. "Vorticism." *Fortnightly Review* ns 573 (1914): 461–71.

Pound, Ezra, and Ernest Fenollosa. *The Classic Noh Theatre of Japan*. New York: New Directions, 1959.

Pratt, William. *The Imagist Poem*. New York: Dutton, 1963.

Sanchez, Sonia. *Like the Singing Coming off the Drums*. Boston: Beacon, 1998.

Sharp, E. A. *William Sharp: A Memoir*. London: Heinemann, 1910.

Shirane, Haruo. *Traces of Dreams: Landscape, Cultural Memory, and the Poetry of Bashō*. Stanford, CA: Stanford University Press, 1998.

Stepto, Robert. *From Behind the Veil: A Study of Afro-American Narrative*. Urbana: University of Illinois Press, 1979.

Stock, Noel. *Poet in Exile: Ezra Pound*. Manchester: Manchester University Press, 1964.

Stoddard, Charles Warren. "Introduction." Yone Noguchi. *The Voice of the Valley*. San Francisco: Doxey, 1897. 10–11.

Teele, Roy E. "The Japanese Translations." *Texas Quarterly* 10 (1967): 61–66.

Thoreau, Henry David. *The Variorum Civil Disobedience.* Ed. Walter Harding. New York: Twayne, 1967.

———. *Walden.* Ed. J. Lyndon Shanley. Princeton, NJ: Princeton University Press, 1971.

———. *A Week on the Concord and Merrimack Rivers.* Ed. Carl F. Hovde et al. Princeton, NJ: Princeton University Press, 1980.

Tonkinson, Carol, ed. *Big Sky Mind: Buddhism and the Beat Generation.* New York: Riverhead, 1995.

Toyama, Usaburo, ed. *Essays on Yone Noguchi.* 3 vols. Tokyo: Zokei Bijutsu Kyokai, 1963.

Twain, Mark. *Adventures of Huckleberry Finn.* Ed. Sculley Bradley et al. New York: Norton, 1977.

Tytell, John. *Naked Angels: The Lives & Literature of the Beat Generation.* New York: McGraw-Hill, 1977.

Ueda, Makoto. *Zeami, Basho, Yeats, Pound: A Study in Japanese and English Poetics.* The Hague: Mouton, 1965.

Waley, Arthur. *The Nō Plays of Japan.* New York: Grove, 1920.

Walker, Margaret. *Richard Wright: Daemonic Genius.* New York: Warner Books, 1988.

Webb, Constance. *Richard Wright: A Biography.* New York: Putnam, 1968.

Werner, Craig. *A Change Is Gonna Come: Music, Race & the Soul of America.* New York: Plume, 1999

———. *Playing the Changes: From Afro-Modernism to the Jazz Impulse.* Urbana: University of Illinois Press, 1994.

Whitman, Walt. *Complete Poetry and Selected Prose.* Ed. James E. Miller, Jr. Boston: Houghton Mifflin, 1959.

———. *Leaves of Grass.* Ed. Sculley Bradley et al. New York: New York University Press, 1980.

Wright, Julia. Introduction. *Haiku: This Other World.* By Richard Wright. Ed. Yoshinobu Hakutani and Robert L. Tener. New York: Arcade, 1998. Rpt. New York: Random House, 2000. vii–xii.

Wright, Richard. *Black Power: A Record of Reactions in a Land of Pathos.* New York: Harper, 1954.

———. "Blueprint for Negro Writing." *Richard Wright Reader.* Ed. Ellen Wright and Michel Fabre. New York: Harper, 1978. 36–49.

———. *Conversations with Richard Wright.* Ed. Keneth Kinnamon and Michel Fabre. Jackson: University Press of Mississippi, 1993.

———. *Haiku: This Other World.* Ed. Yoshinobu Hakutani and Robert L. Tener. New York: Arcade, 1998. Rpt. New York: Random House, 2000.

———. *Native Son.* 1940. New York: Harper & Row, 1966.

———. *Pagan Spain.* New York: Harper and Brothers, 1957.

———. "This Other World: Projections in the Haiku Manner." Ms. New Haven: Beinecke Rare Book and Manuscript Library, Yale University, 1960.

————. *12 Million Black Voices: A Folk History of the Negro in the United States.* New York: Viking, 1941.

Yeats, W. B. *Autobiography.* New York: Macmillan, 1938.

————. "Introduction to *Certain Noble Plays of Japan* by Pound & Fenollosa." *The Classic Noh Theatre of Japan.* New York: New Directions, 1959. 151–63.

————. *The Poems of W. B. Yeats.* Ed. Richard J. Finneran. New York: Macmillan, 1983.

————. *Reveries over Childhood and Youth.* Dublin: Cuala, 1916.

————. *The Variorum Edition of the Plays of W. B. Yeats.* Ed. Russell K. Alspach. New York: Macmillan, 1966.

Youmans, Rich. "For My Wife on Our First Anniversary." *Brussels Sprout* 11.3 (1994): 15.

SUBJECT INDEX

Index of Haiku and Poems

194   INDEX OF HAIKU AND POEMS

POEMS (BY TITLE)